CARLISLE
TO BEATTOCK

Including the Dumfries Branch

Roger Darsley & Dennis Lovett

MP Middleton Press

Front cover: Avanti West Coast class 390 EMU no. 390117 Blue Peter *pauses at Carlisle with the 13.55 for London Euston on 1st June 2021. The train was running almost an hour late due to overhead line problems in the Carstairs area. (D.A.Lovett)*

Back cover picture: Royal Scot class 4-6-0 no. 46118 Royal Welch Fusilier *was passing Beattock North signal box on its way to attack the bank. (R.Barbour/B.McCartney coll.)*

Back cover map: Railway Clearing House map, dated 1947. The route of the album is shown with a dotted line.

Readers of this book may be interested in the following societies:

Caledonian Railway Association
www.crassoc.org.uk

Cumbrian Railway Association
www.cumbrianrailways.org.uk

Scottish Railway Correspondence & Travel Society, Scottish Branch
email: *scotland@rcts.org.uk*

Stephenson Locomotive Society
www.stephensonloco.org.uk

Devil's Porridge Museum
www.devilsporridge.org.uk
Tel: 01461 700021

Published February 2022

ISBN 978 1 910356 69 2

© Middleton Press Ltd, 2022

Cover design Deborah Esher
Design Cassandra Morgan

Published by
Middleton Press Ltd
Camelsdale Road
Haslemere, Surrey
GU27 3RJ
Tel: 01730 813169
Email: info@middletonpress.co.uk
www.middletonpress.co.uk

Printed by Mapseeker Digital Ltd, Unit 15, Bridgwater Court, Oldmixon Crescent, Weston Super Mare, North Somerset, BS24 9AY.   Telephone +44 (0) 01922 458288 +44 (0) 7947107248

CONTENTS

I. Map of the southern end of the Caledonian Railway between Carlisle and Beattock including the branch from Lockerbie to Dumfries.
(A.E.Young)

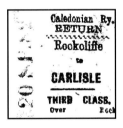

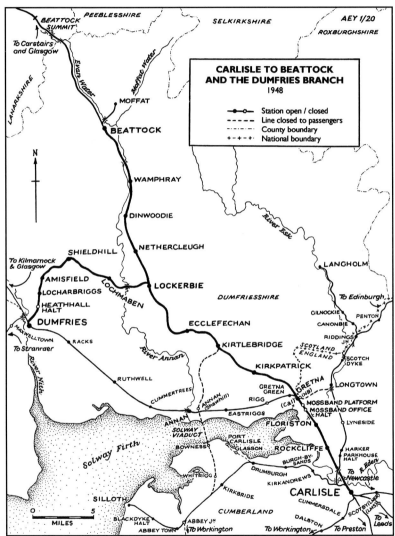

ACKNOWLEDGEMENTS

We are grateful for the assistance received from many of those mentioned in the photographic credits and also to D.Coddington, G.Croughton, G. Gartside, J.Hewitt (Devils Porridge Museum), C.M. Howard, N.Langridge, A.P.McLean, B.Read, D. and Dr S. Salter, J.Turner (Dumfries Museum), J. P. Vickers and J. W. Yellowlees (ScotRail).

GEOGRAPHICAL SETTING

Due to its geology, the Scottish Borders provided just three opportunities to link Carlisle with Scotland's two largest cities (Edinburgh & Glasgow). These are known as the Nithsdale, Annandale and Liddesdale routes. The first, via Dumfries, was later utilised by the Glasgow & South Western Railway (GSWR) and the last by the North British Railway (NBR) via Hawick (covered in our *Carlisle to Hawick* album). Annandale provided the middle route via Lockerbie, Beattock and Carstairs, where lines would diverge to serve both cities.

Carlisle's natural position (10 miles south of the Scottish Border) made it an attractive option for the Romans who built Hadrian's Wall from the Tyne to the Solway Firth into which three rivers, the Eden, the Caldew and the Petteril flow. Carlisle itself lies on a bed of Triassic Red Sandstone and Mudstone.

The Southern Uplands, which run from the Ayrshire coast to the east coast near Dunbar, were formed when sedimentary deposits from the Iapetus Ocean were pushed upwards from the seabed some 400 million years ago during the Caledonian orogeny. Most of the rocks are weakly metamorphosed coarse greywacke.

The line between Carlisle and Lockerbie provides rich arable farmland before the hills begin to rise as the West Coast Main Line follows the valley of the River Annan. Beyond Beattock, the line starts to climb into the Lowther Hills, which form part of the Southern Uplands.

All maps are based on 25ins to 1 mile editions, with north at the top, unless otherwise indicated.

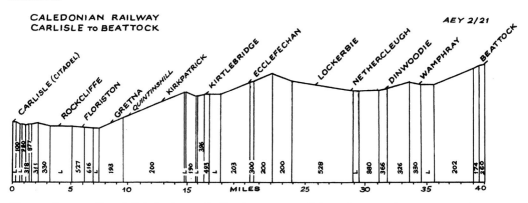

The gradient profile of Caledonian main line between Carlisle and Beattock. (A.E.Young)

HISTORICAL BACKGROUND

The linking of Carlisle and Scotland by rail was first mooted in the *Carlisle Journal* in August 1835. The paper supported the argument for a West Coast Anglo-Scottish route rather than the East Coast one. Shortly afterwards, the Grand Junction Railway, then in process of building a line to Preston, sent its engineer, Joseph Locke, to look at the possibilities. It was deemed at the time that there was financial justification to support only one route and the government-appointed commissioners opted for the East Coast route in 1841.

Those promoting the West Coast option did not give up and by 1843 the Lancaster & Carlisle Railway company (L&CR) was up and running. The Act of Parliament allowing its construction received the Royal Assent on 6th June 1844. By December 1846 rails stretched from London to Carlisle.

The Caledonian Railway (CR) was promoted to link Carlisle with Scotland's two largest cities, Edinburgh and Glasgow. The Annandale route was followed through Lockerbie, and beyond Beattock climbed into the Lowther Hills before descending into the Clyde valley. At Carstairs the lines to Glasgow and Edinburgh split.

The CR received its Act of Parliament on 31st July 1845, with the line between Carlisle and Beattock opening on 10th September 1847. The line north was extended both to Edinburgh and Glasgow on 15th February 1848.

The Glasgow line north of Carstairs terminated at Garriongill, where it formed a junction with the Wishaw & Coltness Railway (W&CR) which, together with the lines of the Glasgow, Garnkirk & Coatbridge Railway (GG&CR) reached Glasgow, the first trains from Carlisle terminating at their Townhead terminus. From 1849 they used the inconvenient terminus South Side that was already in use by the Glasgow, Barrhead and Neilston Direct Railway for a short period. The CR then moved to the north of the city to use its own Buchanan Street terminus by building a new line from Milton Junction (opened 1st November 1849) off the Townhead line. These lines did not remain independent for long, the W&CR becoming part of the CR in 1849 and the GG&CR being leased by the CR in January 1846. The latter was originally a 4ft 6in gauge railway but was converted in August 1847 to standard gauge. The final act of amalgamation took place in June 1865, the GG&CR becoming part of the Caledonian.

The Edinburgh line originally terminated at Lothian Road. After the opening of Princes Street on 2nd May 1879, Lothian Road became a goods station.

Services from Carlisle were transferred to Glasgow Central on its opening in 1879. The station originally had eight platforms with a ninth platform being added in 1890. It was further extended between 1901 and 1905 to 13 platforms with one more being added and another extended in 2010 as part of the now abandoned Glasgow Airport Rail Link. In 2019, the station was used by 106,000 passengers daily equating to some 34 million each year.

The main lines soon became part of the West Coast operation with trains being worked by the London & North Western Railway (LNWR) to Carlisle and from Carlisle north by the CR. Local services from Carlisle to Beattock were the domain of the Caledonian as were the freight workings.

In 1923, the LNWR, CR and the adjacent GSWR, which served Dumfries, became part of the London, Midland & Scottish Railway (LMS) at the Grouping.

During the 1930s the line saw most of the express trains hauled by Stanier's Princess Royal and Princess Coronation Class locomotives. On 16th November 1936, with no. 6201 *Princess Elizabeth* at its head, Driver Tom Clarke, Fireman Charles Fleet and Passed Fireman Albert Shaw reached Glasgow Central in 5 hours 53 minutes 38 seconds on a non-stop run. The following day they did it again in the reverse direction in 5 hours 44 minutes 14 seconds. On arrival the crew were taken to Broadcasting House and interviewed by the BBC and, following a run on the Royal Train on 12th July 1937, Driver Clarke was summoned to the King's coach where he was presented with an OBE (Order of the British Empire) for his role in the runs a year earlier.

Following nationalisation on 1st January 1948, the route passed to the Scottish Region of British Railways with the shed being allocated shed code 68A in the Scottish Region series. Carlisle Kingmoor shed was transferred to the London Midland Region in February 1958 where it became 12A, regaining its former LMS shed code.

By the mid 1960s diesel traction was taking hold and the steam sheds in Scotland lost their allocation of steam locomotives during 1967. Steam continued to be seen in Carlisle during 1968 although the city no longer had its own allocation before British Rail ceased using standard gauge steam traction in August 1968.

It was not long before continuation of the West Coast Main Line electrification scheme was contemplated. Services between London Euston and Liverpool / Manchester were fully electrified by 1966. Electrification between Weaver Junction (north of Crewe where the Liverpool line leaves the West Coast Main Line) and Motherwell / Glasgow was authorised 23rd February 1970 at a cost of £25m covering 235 route miles. Several suburban routes in the Glasgow area had been electrified in the 1960s. The extended electric line opened on 6th May 1974 allowing through services to run with electric traction between London Euston and Glasgow Central for the first time. The final cost of the scheme was some £74m.

Electric services between Carstairs and Edinburgh commenced on 18th March 1991. Electrification of the line from Berwick to Edinburgh was also completed and the first through electric train from London via the East Coast Main Line ran on 12th June 1991.

Following privatisation in 1997, express services on the route north of Carlisle were operated by Virgin Trains West Coast (1997-2019). Services are currently operated by Avanti West Coast, Caledonian Sleeper, CrossCountry and TransPennine Express. Ironically, Lockerbie station is managed by ScotRail from Dumfries, but no ScotRail trains operate on the section of line through Lockerbie!

As part of the West Coast Route Modernisation programme the route was upgraded between 1999 and 2004. A local rail Action Group continues to press for the reopening of Beattock station but there are currently no plans to do so.

All stations covered in this album opened with their respective lines unless otherwise stated.

Dumfries Branch

The line from Lockerbie to Dumfries was initially an independent concern, the Dumfries, Lochmaben & Lockerbie Railway. Supported by the CR the line linked with the GSWR at Dumfries, which had opened its own line from Carlisle in 1848 and extended to Kilmarnock and Glasgow a year later.

It was intended for the 14½-mile line to have its own station in Dumfries, but the GSWR objected, and trains worked into the GSWR station, using the tracks of the Castle Douglas & Dumfries line to share bay platforms at the north end of the station. The site of the intended terminus at St. Mary's became the CR goods station whilst the CR engine shed was also located there.

Authorised on 14th June 1860, the line was opened for traffic on 1st September 1863 and was operated by the Caledonian from the start. For a period between 4th December 1864 and 1st January 1865, the line was used to reach Stranraer, which provided the shortest sea crossing to Ireland (now Northern Ireland). The boat train workings ceased from 1865 and the line reverted to branch line status.

The Grouping in 1923 saw both the CR and the GSWR fall under the same ownership, becoming part of the LMS. This allowed closure of the CR engine shed with all locomotive activity taking place at the former GSWR facility at Dumfries.

Regular passenger traffic was withdrawn on 19th May 1952 although some rail tours ran until closure to all traffic on 18th April 1966. The trackbed between Locharbriggs and Dumfries is now in use as a cycle path.

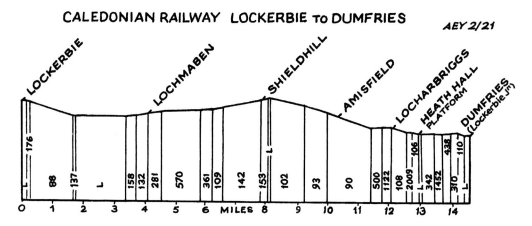

The gradient profile of the Lockerbie - Dumfries line. (A.E. Young)

PASSENGER SERVICES

On the opening of the line on 10th September 1847 the timetable covered only the 39½ miles between Carlisle and Beattock (the line north not opening until February 1848). Journey time was two hours and the service consisted of three trains a day in each direction serving all intermediate stations, apart from Kirtlebridge, which was not opened until the following year.

By 1947 local all-stations trains took 1 hour 15 minutes to travel between Carlisle and Beattock whilst express trains took 56 minutes with an intermediate stop at Lockerbie. There were three local services a day in each direction, although there were some nine northbound departures a day from Lockerbie and 13 from Beattock.

There are currently 20 down and 22 up trains between Carlisle and Lockerbie provided by Anglo-Scottish trains operated by TransPennine Express. Journey time is on average 18 minutes. Lockerbie is the only intermediate station to remain on the route, although reopening of Beattock is high on the agenda of rail campaigners in Scotland.

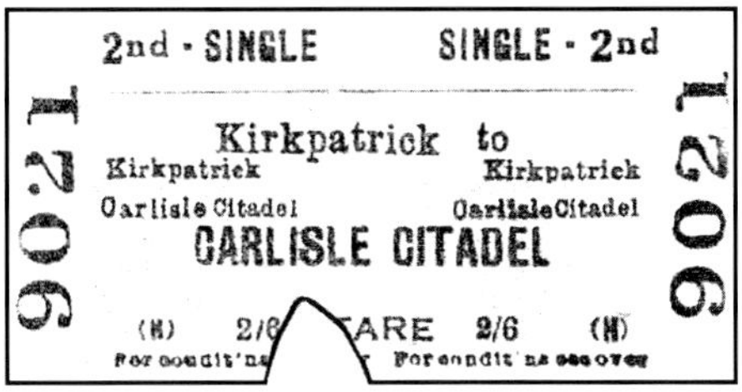

The down timetable for Summer 1918.

LONDON, CARLISLE, EDINBURGH, GLASGOW, STIRLING, OBAN, PERTH, INVERNESS, MONTROSE, and ABERDEEN.—Caledonian.

Offices—302, Buchanan Street, Glasgow. Gen. Man., Donald A. Matheson. Supt. of the Line, R. Killin. Sec., John Blackburn.

Week Days.

Miles from Carlisle	Down.	mrn	aft	mrn	mrn	mrn	mrn	mrn	mrn	mrn	mrn	aft		aft	aft	mrn	mrn	mrn	mrn	mrn	mrn	mrn	mrn	mrn	aft	aft	aft	non	aft
	428 London (Euston) dep.		7 20									8 55		8 35	1130														11 40
	576 " (St. Pan.) "													8 45															
	428 Birmingham § "		8 5											10p55															2r55
	448 Liverpool (L. St.) "		1040											12 45															
	448 " (Exchange) "													1 50															
	448 Manchester (V.) "													mrn															
	448 " (Exchange) "		1050											1 15															
		mrn	mrn	mrn	mrn	mrn	mrn	mrn	mrn	mrn	mrn	mrn		mrn	mrn	mrn	mrn	mrn	mrn	mrn	mrn		mrn	mrn	aft	aft	aft	non	mrn
—	Carlisle dep.		2 30									3 55		4 55	7 10							Leaves Moffat at 7 28 mrn, see page 914.	8 35						10 0
4	Rockcliffe												Sleeping Saloon, London (Euston) to Glasgow.																
6	Floriston																						8 47						
8¼	Gretna 842																						8 56						
13	Kirkpatrick		Except Mondays.												Sleeping Saloons, London (Euston) to Glasgow.								9 4						
16¼	Kirtlebridge ‡ 925																						9 14						10 24
20	Ecclefechan																						9 22						
25¾	Lockerbie 925											4X33		5 32									9 32						10 42
28¾	Nethercleugh																						9 42						
31¾	Dinwoodie																						9 49						
34½	Wamphray																						9 57						11 6
39¾	Beattock 914											4X55		5 55								7 35	10 8						11 8
52¾	Elvanfoot 915																					7 57	Runs to Moffat, arriving at 10 16 mrn, see page 914.						11 27
55½	Crawford																					8 3							11 44
57¾	Abington																					8 8							11 50
63¼	Lamington																					8 15							12 0
66¾	Symington 927 arr.																					8 21							12 6
	dep.																					8 24							12 8
68½	Thankerton 926																					8 31							12 18
73½	Carstairs 924, 925, arr.											5X54		6 46								8 39							12 28
101	925 Edinbro' (Prn. St.) arr.																					9 33							1 47
—	Carstairs dep.													6 50								8 45							12 36
76½	Cleghorn																												
80¼	Braidwood																												
82	Carluke																					8 58							12 54
84	Law Junction arr.													Fp															1 1
	dep.																												1 3
86½	Wishaw (South)																												1 8
88¼	Flemington																												1 13
89½	Motherwell 914 arr.											6X24		7 25								9 13							1 17
—	Motherwell dep.												7 30									9 31							2 22
91	Mossend																					9 36							2 28
93½	914 Whifflet (Low Level)																					9 43							2 35
94½	909 Coatbridge 915 arr.												7 40									9 45							2 39
—	Motherwell dep.													7t45								9t14							1 20
92¾	Fallside												Through Train to the North.																
93¾	Uddingston 904, 923																												1 34
95½	Newton																												
97¼	Cambuslang																												
99¼	Rutherglen 918																												Aa
101¼	Eglinton Street 908, 910																												1 50
102¼	Glasgow (C.) 904, 906, arr.											6 55		8t20	9 42							9t36							2 0
125¼	908 Greenock (Cen.) arr.											8 38		9 25	1139							1139							4 3
128¼	908 Gourock "											8 53		9 41	1157							1157							4 20
—	Glasgow (Buch. St.) dep.				4g45				5 50	7 0									Leaves Denny at see page		9 45	Stop		1025				12 0	
—	St. Rollox								5 54																				
—	Steps Road								6 5																				
—	Garnkirk **								6 9															1039					
—	Gartcosh								6 13															1043					

For Local Trains and intermediate Stations

BETWEEN	PAGE
Carstairs and Edinburgh	925
Edinburgh (Waverley) and Larbert	851

***** For other Trains**

BETWEEN	PAGE
Edinburgh and Stirling	848
Carlisle and Glasgow	876
Carstairs & Glasgow (Cen.)	913
Motherwell & Coatbridge	909, 915
Whifflet and Coatbridge	915
Motherwell and Glasgow	909, 915
Fallside and Glasgow	913, 923
Uddingston and Glasgow	904, 923
Newton and Glasgow	920
Glasgow (Buchanan Street) and Gartcosh	908
Glasgow and Stirling	849
Glasgow and Perth	849
Glasgow and Aberdeen	844
Carlisle and Edinburgh	842
Edinburgh and Perth	850
Edinburgh and Aberdeen	844
Perth and Stanley	836
Coupar Angus and Ardler	928
Bridge of Dun and Dubton	903

Dumfries Branch

The Caledonian Railway 1918 timetable, below, for the branch line from Lockerbie to Dumfries.

DUMFRIES and LOCKERBIE.—Caledonian.

Miles	Up.	mrn	aft	aft	aft	Miles	Down.	mrn	mrn	aft	aft	aft	aft
	Dumfries ....dep.	8 40	1 0	6 50			Lockerbie ....dep.	7 26	1020	1 45	6 17	7 e 55	8 s 5	
2¼	Locharbriggs.........	8 50	1 7	6 59		4½	Lochmaben	7 30	1028	1 55	6 24	8 e 38	8 s 13	
4½	Amisfield	8 56	1 13	7 8		7½	Shieldhill	7 40	1037	2 5	6 33	8 e 13	8 s 23	
7	Shieldhill...........	9 2	1 19	7 15		10¼	Amisfield	7 49	1044	2 14	6 41	8 e 21	8 s 31	
10½	Lochmaben	9 11	1 28	7 26		12	Locharbriggs.........	8 56	7 54	1049	2 19	6 45	8 e 26	7 s 36
14½	Lockerbie 890, 897...arr.	9 23	1 41	7 40		14½	Dumfries 876, 877, arr.	8 7	11 0	2 32	6 55	8 e 45	8 s 47

e Except Saturdays.   s Saturdays only.

The 1922 Caledonian timetable (not shown) includes six down trains and five up (towards Lockerbie) working passenger trains over the branch. The 1947 LMS timetable, shown below, records a reduction in the service with four down and three up trains in operation. Five years later it would see the withdrawal of all passenger services.

Table 335 — LOCKERBIE and DUMFRIES

Miles		a.m	p.m E	p.m S	p.m	p.m	Miles		a.m	p.m	p.m	p.m	p.m
	Lockerbie.........dep	7 37	1 20	1 26	6 22	8 20	—	Dumfries..........dep	6 38	1220	1240	4 25	7 28
4½	Lochmaben	7 48	1 28	1 34	6 30	8 28	2¼	Locharbriggs		1227	1247	4 32	7 35
7½	Shieldhill...........	7 57	1 34	1 40	6 36	8 34	4½	Amisfield	6 Å47	1233	1253	4 38	7 42
10½	Amisfield..........	8 5	1 42	1 48	6 44	8 42	7	Shieldhill...........		1239	1259	4 44	7 49
12	Locharbriggs	8 9	1 47	1 53	6 50	8 49	10½	Lochmaben	7 0	1248	1 8	4 53	7 58
14½	Dumfries..........arr	8 16	1 56	2 6	6 57	8 57	14½	Lockerbie..........arr	7 7	1256	1 16	5 1	8 7

Å Calls to take up on notice being given to the Station Master on previous day
E Except Saturdays.   S Saturdays only.

The TransPennine Express down timetable for 2019-20 is shown below. Lockerbie is the only station between Carlisle and Carstairs to remain open. Although a staffed ScotRail station, it has no ScotRail trains running between Carlisle and Carstairs. TransPennine Express is the main operator to stop there with Avanti West Coast providing one train a day in each direction to and from London Euston.

CARLISLE CITADEL

II.   The City of Carlisle was home to several railways each with its own terminal station around its edge. The first line to reach it was from Newcastle arriving in 1836. By the time this 1899 map was published, Carlisle's railway infrastructure was complete.

The Caledonian (CR) and Lancaster & Carlisle (L&CR) companies - later London & North Western (LNWR) agreed to build a joint station close to the castle and the city centre. It takes its name Citadel from the adjacent medieval fortress and was completed by the time the two companies had constructed their lines into Carlisle, which was in September 1847. The station was designed by Sir William Tite (1798-1873) whose architectural work included several well-known railway stations. Eventually other companies utilised Citadel station, including the Newcastle & Carlisle and the Maryport & Carlisle and, in 1857, Carlisle came under the control of a joint management committee. They would later be joined by the North British (NBR) and Glasgow & South Western (GSWR) railway companies.

A seventh company, the Midland (MR) reached the city in 1876 with the completion of the Settle & Carlisle line. It provided express trains from London both to Edinburgh and Glasgow in partnership with the North British (to Edinburgh via Hawick) and the Glasgow & South Western (to Glasgow via Dumfries and Kilmarnock).

Carlisle was enlarged between 1873 and 1876 and again between 1878 and 1881 to accommodate more trains. It is now a Grade 2 listed building.

This map is based on a 6in to 1 mile map, but has been reduced in scale to approximately 2in to 1 mile.

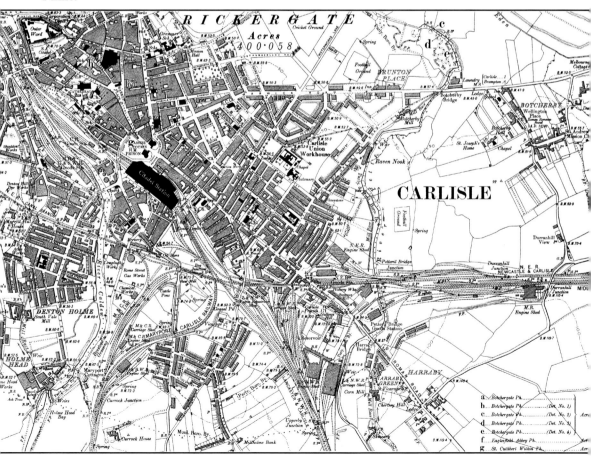

1. The exterior of Carlisle Citadel station as it was on 1st June 2021. Built in 1847 it served seven railway companies. The NBR acquired access in October 1861, the NER in January 1863 and the MR in 1876. The platforms and glass roof were restored between 2015 and 2018. (D.A.Lovett)

2. Princess Royal class 4-6-2 no. 46203 *Princess Margaret Rose* was hauling a southbound express on 8th May 1958 and entered the station under the Victoria Viaduct. (R.S.Carpenter)

3.   Jubilee class 4-6-0 no. 45707 *Valiant* and A3 class 4-6-2 no. 60035 *Windsor Lad* are seen after the arrival of the up 'Waverley Express' on 8th May 1958. No. 45707 will take the train south over the Settle & Carlisle line to London St. Pancras. (R.S.Carpenter)

4.   'Black 5' 5MT 4-6-0 no. 44706 was on the 10.40 departure for Glasgow St. Enoch by the GSWR line. The date was 27th April 1949, and the war-time grime is evident at this end of the station. (H.C.Casserley)

5.   Carlisle was a good station for seeing engine changeovers. Here, in April 1982, is a line-up of two 1-Co-Co-1 DE (diesel electric) class 45s with no. 45026 standing at platform 4 and an unidentified locomotive standing on the centre road. A class 86 Bo-Bo WE (wire electric) is heading north up the West Coast Main Line to Glasgow. (P.Barnes)

6.   Prior to electrification, double heading was commonplace to avoid the use of banking engines over the Shap and Beattock summits. On 28th August 1971, English Electric Co-Co DE D400 class (later class 50) nos 401 and 422 are taking a train from London Euston north to Glasgow Central. (T.Heavyside)

7.   Haymarket-based BRCW Type 2 Bo-Bo DE (later class 26) no. D5312 leaves with the 13.00 service to Edinburgh Waverley via Hawick on 7th December 1968, just a month before the Waverley route closed to passenger traffic. (K.A.Gray/B.McCartney coll.)

8.   An unidentified class 156 DMU in Strathclyde livery was in platform 7, one of the bay platforms once used by Waverley route trains. It awaits departure for Glasgow Central over the GSWR route via Dumfries and Kilmarnock during June 2002. (D.A.Lovett)

9.   On 27th February 2012, two preserved stalwarts of the early electrification period were in the locomotive sidings, formerly used as carriage sidings. Class 86 Bo-Bo WE no. 86101 *Sir William A Stanier FRS* and class 87 Bo-Bo no. 87002 *Royal Sovereign* pose for the camera. (D.A.Lovett)

10.   Freight comes through the station following the loss of the Citadel-avoiding lines in 1984. At 12.33 on 3rd July 2009 class 66/0 Co-Co DE no. 66082 in EWS livery hauls a rake of Rail Freight Services, branded FCA bogie wagons as an additional 'Enterprise' service from Carlisle Yard to Tees Yard. (B.E.Morrison)

11.   Virgin Trains were the first franchise holders to operate both the West Coast Main Line and CrossCountry after privatisation and here are two CrossCountry units carrying their livery. HST with power car no. 43094 and 43121 at the rear heads the 13.17 departure to Penzance. Super Voyager class 221 no. 221104 *Sir John Franklin* waits on platform 3 with the 13.25 to Bournemouth on 21st June 2003.(R.R.Darsley)

12.   Virgin Trains lost the franchise to Avanti West Coast in December 2019. There was an interval in which the class 390 Pendolino trains appeared in neutral grey following the removal of the Virgin Trains branding. Both the 13.12 up train and the Glasgow train on platform 3 are carrying this livery on 24th February 2020. (D.A.Lovett)

13. TransPennine Express 'Nova 2' class 397 no. 397005, a five-car EMU, is in a centre road, at the south end of Carlisle, with a test train for Manchester Airport via Preston on 1st June 2021. (D.A.Lovett)

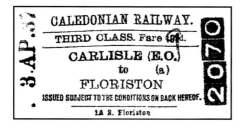

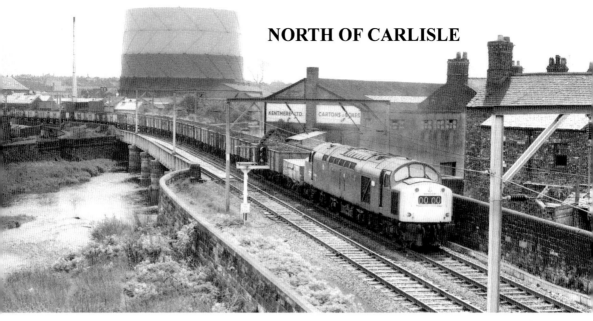

14. Class 40 1-Co-Co-1 no. 40198 was hauling a coke train north across the River Calder bridge on 16th May 1977. These avoiding lines were used until 1984 when a Freightliner train derailed on the bridge and brought down a span. The bridge was not rebuilt. (T. Heavyside)

15. This photograph is of Dentonholme North Junction seen here on a misty morning. The avoiding lines came in from the right. West Walls Engine Shed was on the far left but was closed in 1877 and no photographs of it have yet been found. (H.C.Casserley)

West Walls Engine Shed

➔ 16.   Princess Coronation class 4-6-2 no. 46240 *City of Coventry* was on the up 'Caledonian' passing the cathedral's west walls. The 'Caledonian' was usually a Princess Coronation working. (B.Brooksbank/Geograph 2414901)

III. This 1874 map, scaled at approximately 12in to 1 mile, shows the engine shed at West Walls and its proximity to Trinity Cathedral, just to the north of Citadel station. This was the second CR shed that had opened in 1849 having replaced an earlier temporary single-road facility at the North end of the station, although we have been unable to identify its location. This had opened with the line two years earlier and accommodated both Caledonian and Glasgow & South Western locomotives.

The West Walls facility, as it was known locally (and occasionally officially), was the cause of considerable annoyance to the Dean of Carlisle who had to live adjacent to both the noise and smoke that it produced. The Cathedral dates from 1133 when Carlisle also achieved city status. On at least one occasion, the church took to the courts to restore some balance and there must have been considerable ecclesiastical rejoicing when the shed was removed to Etterby, to the north of the city, in 1877 to establish what later became Kingmoor. In 1886 the shed was demolished. The site then became derelict, again to the annoyance of many. The site was later landscaped and is now Town Dyke car park.

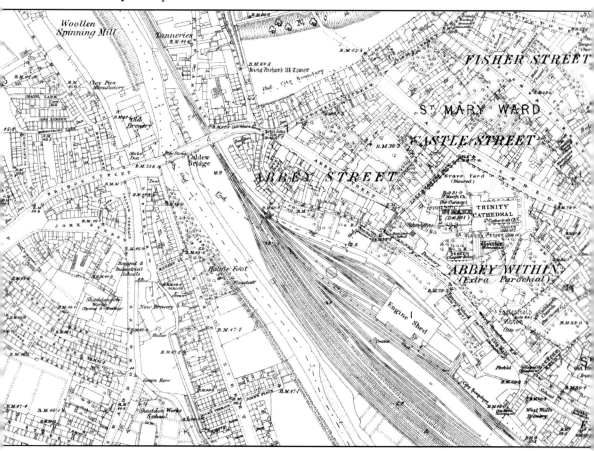

Etterby Bridge

17.   'Black 5' 4-6-0 no. 44850 crosses the River Eden at Etterby on a northbound parcels train on 4th July 1959. A light engine passes on the 1942-built bridge that carries the goods lines. It is awaiting the signal to allow it to proceed to Kingmoor Locomotive Sheds. (R.Barbour/B.McCartney coll.)

18.   Class 40 1-Co-Co-1 no. 40135 heads north over the River Eden with a train for Kingmoor Yard on 16th May 1977. Carlisle Cathedral and Castle are visible on the horizon. (T.Heavyside)

Etterby Junction

IV.   Located on the north bank of the River Eden, which is crossed by a viaduct, the junction opened in 1874 to serve the construction of the new engine shed, then in the process of being relocated from West Walls. The junction was controlled by the signal box located on the west side opposite the southern entrance to the shed, the northern access being controlled from Kingmoor Junction. The junction and its approaches are seen here in 1924, in this 12in to 1 mile extract. The box was taken out of use in 1963 when Kingmoor Power Box was commissioned.

19.   On 13th June 2014, class 390 Pendolino no. 390155 in XMEN livery is on the 13.40 Glasgow Central to London Euston service. This unit was named at Euston on 31st March 2014 in conjunction with the launch of the film 'XMEN – Days of Future Past'. (G.W.Morrison)

Kingmoor Shed

20. Map IV, opposite picture 18, shows the extensive facilities provided at Kingmoor; the Caledonian shed to the north of the city. Opened in August 1877 it replaced the previous facility at West Walls. The land had been acquired as early as 1857 to block the CR's great rival, the NBR, which planned to approach the city from Hawick. Some sidings were set out on acquisition but there was no traffic to fill them. The North British 'Waverley Route' is on the left-hand side of the map on its way to crossing the West Coast Main Line en route to Hawick and Edinburgh. This line was covered in our *Carlisle to Hawick* album.

Construction commenced in 1874 and the facility was in limited use by 1876. Etterby, as it was then known, fully opened in August 1877. Major development took place from 1891 when the depot name changed to Kingmoor and a new shed building on the site of the old one was completed during World War I and comprised a double-ended eight-road shed.

At its peak, some 140 locomotives were allocated to Kingmoor. It was coded 12A in LMS days but following nationalisation in 1948, Carlisle became a Scottish Region shed despite its location some 8½ miles south of the border, becoming 68A. It was transferred to the London Midland Region in 1958, reverting to its LMS code of 12A.

Following closure of the sheds at Durranhill in 1936, Canal in 1963 and Upperby in 1966, Kingmoor was the last of the steam sheds to serve Carlisle. The shed closed on 31st December 1967 following the end of Scottish steam working, but, with steam concentrated in the northwest of England for its remaining eight months on British Railways, steam was still working into the city until the end in August 1968. The shed was replaced by the opening of a new diesel depot on the opposite side of the tracks. The shed buildings were demolished, and the site returned to nature. Today much of the former Kingmoor shed site is a wildlife haven although the former loco staff hostel at the south end of the site remains in use as private residential accommodation.

The display of 14 4-4-0 'Dunalastairs' of the first and second series had worked a mammoth sequence of excursion trains, taking the staff of St Rollox Works, Glasgow, for a day out in Carlisle. (Locomotive Publishing Co./R.M.Casserley coll.)

21.   In LMS livery and numbered 14644, this Pickersgill designed 4-6-0 had moved away from the design of the McIntosh 901 class. The date was 27th May 1936, and the locomotive is at the north end of the shed with the coaling tower in the background. Built in 1926, it was withdrawn in April 1948, the class being nicknamed 'greybacks'. (R.J.Bradley/Initial Photographics)

22.   This is a more general view of the shed. The nearest locomotive is Britannia class 4-6-2 no. 70013 *Oliver Cromwell*, which took part in the last BR steam-hauled excursions at the end of main line steam in August 1968, including the '15 Guinea Special'. As a result, it was preserved as part of the National Collection and at the time of writing was located on the Great Central Railway in Leicestershire. (H.C.Casserley)

23.   Princess Coronation class 4-6-2 no. 46226 *Duchess of Norfolk* and BR Standard Clan class 4-6-2 no. 72009 *Clan Stewart* stand underneath the coaling plant on 6th April 1963. (G.W.Morrison)

24.   It is 27th August 1967 and there were 105 locomotives present that day even though it is just four months to go before the steam depot was closed. Present were two 'Black 5' 4-6-0s, nos 44928 and 45120, both of which appear to be out of use. (W.Jamieson)

25.   The depot turntable was at the far end of the depot yard. Princess Royal class 4-6-2 no. 46201 *Princess Elizabeth* was being turned on 7th June 1962. This locomotive ran non-stop between London Euston and Glasgow Central on 16th November 1936 and completed the non-stop run back to Euston the following day. It was withdrawn from Carlisle Upperby shed in October 1962. The locomotive was bought for preservation and is often seen working the 'Northern Belle' on the West Coast Main Line. (K.Gray/B.McCartney coll.)

Kingmoor Diesel Depot

V.   With the end of standard gauge steam traction drawing near, work began on a new diesel depot early in 1967. It was officially opened on 1st January 1968, the day after Kingmoor ceased to have an allocation of steam locomotives. In 1973 it lost its 12A shed code becoming KM, which was changed to KD from January 1975 until closure in 1987.

The depot remained derelict until 1998, when work began to provide a facility for Direct Rail Services (DRS) who rebuilt it. The new shed immediately south of Kingmoor Yard, was reopened in 2000 and remains the operational base of DRS with full servicing and maintenance facilities. The depot's KM designation returned in 2000. The diagram shows the track layout at the time of going to press. (A.E.Young)

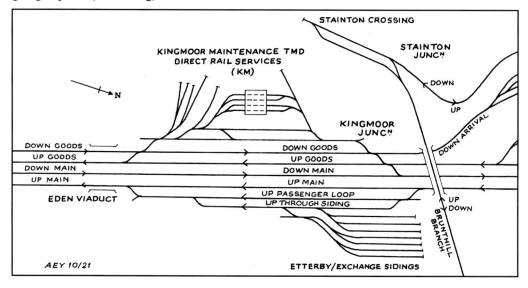

STAINTON CROSSING

KINGMOOR MAINTENANCE TMD
DIRECT RAIL SERVICES
(KM)

STAINTON
JUNCⁿ

→N

DOWN

UP

KINGMOOR
JUNCⁿ

DOWN ARRIVAL

DOWN GOODS
UP GOODS
DOWN MAIN
UP MAIN

EDEN VIADUCT

DOWN GOODS
UP GOODS
DOWN MAIN
UP MAIN
UP PASSENGER LOOP
UP THROUGH SIDING

UP
DOWN

BRUNTHILL
BRANCH

AEY 10/21

ETTERBY/EXCHANGE SIDINGS

26.   TMD stands for Traction Maintenance Depot. This was built on the opposite side of the line from the steam depot. Three members of the first generation of heavy diesel power locomotives were inside the shed during an open day in April 1971. In the foreground is no. D267; the other two are unidentified. The Class 40 1-Co-Co-1 DE locomotives were built between 1958 and 1962. Eight members of the class have been preserved. (J.Furneval)

27.   Another open day with the depot under new management on 7th July 2007. DRS (Direct Rail Services) was established in 1995 by British Nuclear Fuels and are currently part of the Nuclear Decommissioning Authority, a government-owned organisation. Originally, they hauled nuclear waste from power stations to Sellafield for which Class 20 Bo-Bo DE locomotives working in tandem were ideal. In this view, two Class 20 Bo-Bo DE are outside whilst two Class 66 Co-Co DE and a Class 37 Co-Co DE are in the shed. (D.A.Lovett)

← 28.   Open days are rare these days, but this one was held on 22nd July 2009. From left to right were class 66 Co-Co DE no. 66431, class 57's Co-Co DE nos 57007 and 57011. On the jacks was class 37 Co-Co DE no. 37603. The class 57s were rebuilt with EMD (Electro-Motive Diesel) engines fitted to former class 47 locomotives by Brush at Loughborough. (B.McCartney)

↙ 29.   DRS developed contracts with companies and produced locomotives in special liveries to reflect their on-going relationship. Class 66 Co-Co DE no. 66411 *Eddie the Engine* is in Stobart Rail livery of blue, red, white and green, with the name reflecting the Carlisle-based logistics company founded by Eddie Stobart in 1970. Behind is no. 66405 in the dark blue of Malcolm Logistics Services, seen here on 7th July 2007. (D.A.Lovett)

Kingmoor Yard

VI.   This simplified schematic diagram shows the yard on its opening in 1963. There were several yards around Carlisle, which meant frequent trip working between them for marshalling into trains for elsewhere.

As part of the British Railways Modernisation Plan, a new yard at Kingmoor was commissioned to replace them. This included the existing up and down yards at Kingmoor. Work began in later 1959 on the £5m scheme to provide 101 sorting sidings, 18 reception sidings and 20 departure sidings, which were required to handle some 238 trains a day. The yard was commissioned on 5th June 1963 with other yards in the city closing shortly afterwards.

Although it remains in use, hump shunting has ceased, and the yard is much smaller today than depicted on the map. (British Railways)

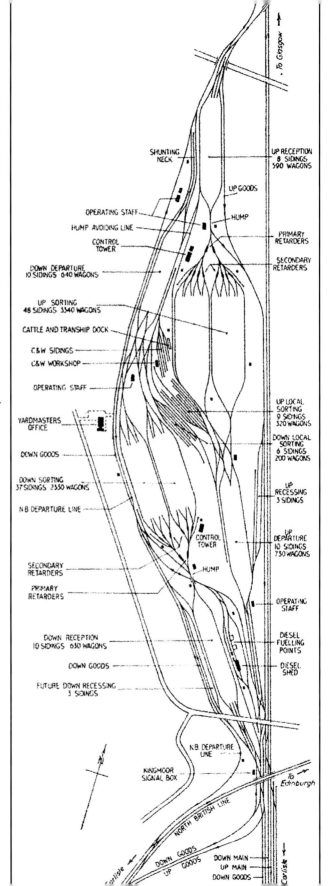

30.　Class 40 1-Co-Co-1 no. 40064 arrives at Kingmoor Yard from the south on 30th August 1979 whilst an up car train passes on the West Coast Main Line. In the background is the bridge carrying the old Waverley route over the yard and the main line. It ran to Edinburgh via Hawick and Galashiels. (G.W.Morrison)

31.　Former NBR K Class 4-4-0 (later LNER D34) no. 256 *Glen Douglas* pauses in Kingmoor Yard for a photo stop on 6th April 1963 whilst working the SLS/MLS (Stephenson Loco. Society/ Manchester Loco. Society) Carlisle Rail Tour. In the background is the yard control tower. No. 256 is now an exhibit at the Riverside Museum, Glasgow. (K.A.Gray/B.McCartney coll.)

32. A Brush Type 4 (later class 47) Co-Co DE was leaving the yard with a southbound freight in pre-electrification days. In the background is the yard's own diesel servicing shed. This is where locomotives could be serviced and refuelled ready to await their return workings. (J.Furneval)

33. Here was another freight arriving from the south with a mixed load on 15th May 1977. This train is hauled by class 40 1-Co-Co-1 no. 40176 and the photograph was taken post-electrification. Part of Kingmoor signal box is just visible on the right. (T.Heavyside)

34. Part of the yard is now occupied by a timber-processing plant. Hopes that the Waverley route would be put back as a long siding to serve Kielder Forest, which supplies the timber, have yet to be fulfilled. Class 57/3 no. 57311 *Parker* heads a timber train to Chirk on 12th February 2008. The class 57/3 were designed as rescue engines and for working class 390 Pendolinos along the non-electrified North Wales coast line to Holyhead. The 15 Virgin Trains locomotives were all named after characters from the 'Thunderbirds' TV series, Parker being the chauffeur of Lady Penelope. (G.W.Morrison)

Kingmoor New Yard Diesel Depot

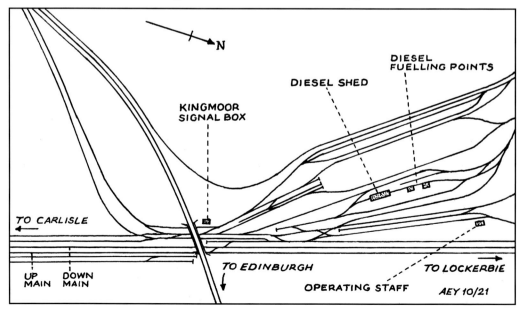

VII.   A single-road diesel inspection shed was provided at the south end of the yard alongside the down reception siding for locomotives working in and out of Kingmoor Yard. It was officially referred to as the F&I facility (Fuelling and Inspection). Its depot code initially was KD, before becoming KM in January 1975. This facility closed around 1987 and was subsequently demolished. (A.E.Young)

35.   There is a mixed collection of locomotives waiting to pick up freight trains from the yard. Identifiable are class 50 Co-Co DE no. D449, built by English Electric, and with them are British Railways constructed class 25 Bo-Bo DE nos D7584 and D5298 on 20th September 1967. (R.S.Carpenter)

36.   The derelict shed stands in a run-down yard in April 2007. The view is looking north with a class 220 DMU in Virgin livery passing on the down line. Virgin called them 'Voyagers' and they carried names of places they served. (J.Furneval)

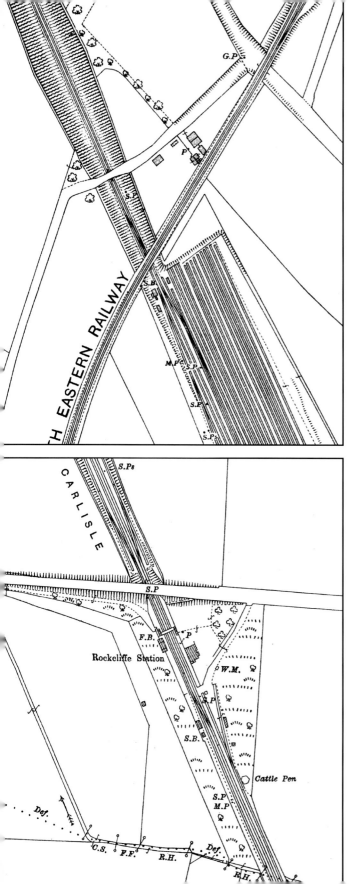

Kingmoor Junction

VIII. Kingmoor Junction, seen here in 1939, was located just south of the bridge carrying the LNER 'Waverley Route' over the West Coast Main Line. The junction controlled by its own signal box gave access to the sidings and shed at Kingmoor following its construction between 1874 and 1877. The box remained in use until 1963 when it was closed and its duties transferred to Kingmoor Power Box.

Caledonian Railway.
Return Half.

FIRST CLASS.
Rockcliffe
TO
CARLISLE(E.O.)
OVER. 1(a) Re

459

ROCKCLIFFE

IX. Seen here in this 1926 map is the station at Rockcliffe, which opened on 10th September 1847. It was located 4 miles north of Carlisle. Like many stations across the country, there was a temporary wartime closure in World War I between 1st January 1917 and 2nd December 1919. For a period in 1921-22 it was renamed Rockcliffe Platform. Closure both to passenger and goods traffic took place on 17th July 1950. However, the passenger station remained open for railway staff and was renamed Rockcliffe Halt serving the nearby Kingmoor Marshalling Yards, which were constructed between 1959 and 1963. The halt finally closed to workmen's trains on 6th December 1965.

In 1918, the line north of Rockcliffe was quadrupled to the next station at Floriston which resulted in a new signal box being provided to replace that shown in the map. Along with other signal boxes in the area, it closed in 1963 when operations were transferred to Kingmoor Power Box. The tracks north of the former station have been reduced to double line with the former station building remaining in residential use.

37.   This view, taken by November 1911, shows the platforms towards the north. (J.Alsop coll.)

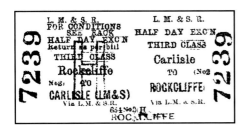

38.   Class 66 Co-Co DE no. 66565 was passing the site of the station on 15th April 2008 with a northbound train of empty coal wagons. The much-modified station building is in residential use and stands on the cut-back embankment of the up platform. The lights of Kingmoor Yard are in the background to the right of the train. (J.Furneval)

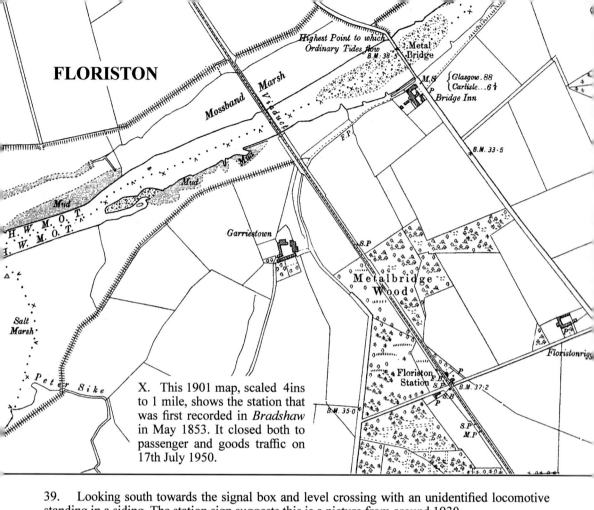

FLORISTON

Highest Point to which
Ordinary Tides flow
B.M. 38·5

Metal
Bridge

Mossband   Marsh   Viaduct

M.S. { Glasgow . 88
      { Carlisle . . . 6¼
P
Bridge Inn

B.M. 33·5

Mud

Mud

H.W.M.O.T.
L.W.M.O.T.

Garriestown

S.P.

Metalbridge
Wood

Salt
Marsh

Floristonrigg

Peter Sike

X. This 1901 map, scaled 4ins
to 1 mile, shows the station that
was first recorded in *Bradshaw*
in May 1853. It closed both to
passenger and goods traffic on
17th July 1950.

Floriston
Station S.P.
B.M. 37·2

B.M. 35·0

S.B

S.P.
M.P.

39.   Looking south towards the signal box and level crossing with an unidentified locomotive
standing in a siding. The station sign suggests this is a picture from around 1930.
(Railway Station Photographs)

FLORISTON

40. Floriston had water troughs to allow engines to pick up water without stopping. Alongside the troughs was a water tank that kept the troughs full. (J.Alsop coll.)

41. Passing under a bridge close to the site of the station was 9F class 2-10-0 no. 92021. This was probably the most successful of the BR Standard class of locomotives with 251 built. Within that number were 10 experimental engines with Crosti boilers. There were two boilers, a pre-heater below the main one. The exhaust, as a result, came out halfway down the locomotive. No. 92021 was new to Wellingborough in May 1955 and converted to a conventional boilered engine in June 1960. It spent a few months at Kettering before being transferred to Kingmoor in June 1964. It moved to Birkenhead in 1965, from where it was withdrawn in 1967. (R.Barbour/B.McCartney coll.)

MOSSBAND OFFICE HALT & PLATFORM

XI.   During World War I, factories were established in the Gretna area to produce Cordite for the Ministry of Munitions. It was code named 'Moorside.'

Stretching for nine miles it consisted of four separate production facilities at Gretna, Smalmstown, Eastriggs and Mossband. Construction commenced in late 1915 and included the building of two wooden townships to house the workers, and the site was operational and producing munitions by April 1916. Other workers were recruited from Carlisle and were transported to the site by train for which two temporary and basic halts were constructed. The down platform known as Mossband Platform was located adjacent to a loop line and was used only for workers' trains that terminated there and was not passed for any other passenger workings. The up platform, known as Mossband Office Halt, was adjacent to the up line. Both were linked to the site by paths. Each platform was 700ft long, 20ft wide and 3ft high and the Office Halt appears to have had a basic shelter. They were inspected and approved for use on 22nd May 1916. Additional sidings and a new signal box with 27 working and 5 spare levers were provided at the same time.

The sites were linked by a 60cm (1.97ft) narrow gauge railway system that employed 34 locomotives working over 125 miles of track in addition to the standard gauge links. Such facilities required a plentiful supply of water from the River Esk and included a coal-fired power station and pumping stations to supply water to where it was needed. The two wooden townships at Eastriggs and Gretna were provided with facilities including a laundry, bakery and their own police force.

By 1917, over 11,000 women and 5,000 men were employed across the sites around Gretna producing cordite. This deadly explosive was manufactured by kneading nitro-glycerine with gun-cotton; over 800 tons a week were produced. This was dangerous material, hence the need to build facilities away from populated areas. Sir Arthur Conan Doyle, the creator of the Sherlock Holmes novels, who was working as a war correspondent, visited the works and dubbed the output 'Devils Porridge'.

Not surprisingly following the cessation of hostilities in November 1918, production finished and some of the manufacturing buildings were demolished. Others remained for storage and parts were sold off for other uses including the two created towns of Gretna and Eastriggs. Some of the site was used during World War II and remains in use for military purposes.

The two halts were quickly removed following the Armistice and the various railway sidings and junctions were removed during the mid-1920s. (A.E.Young)

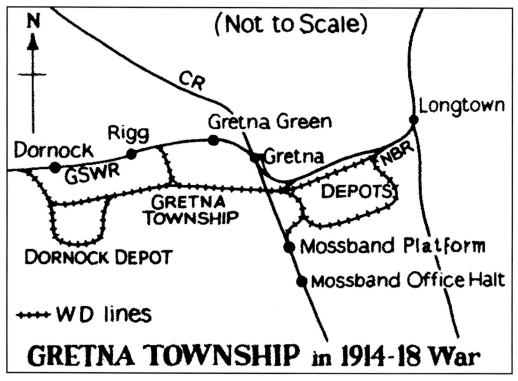

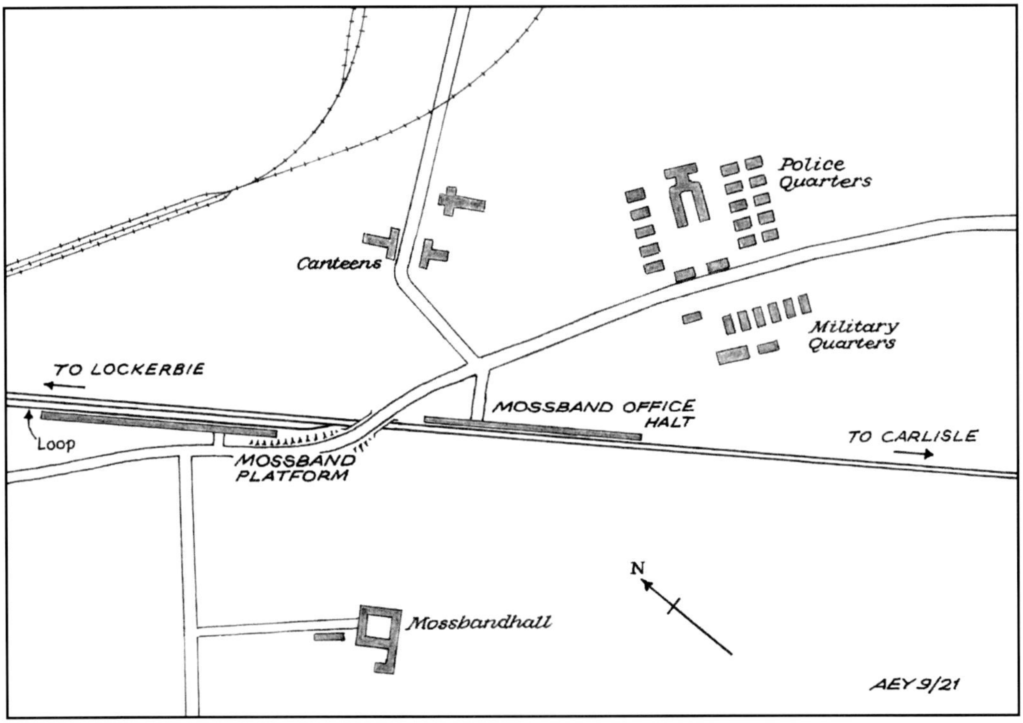
Police
Quarters
Canteens
Military
Quarters
TO LOCKERBIE
MOSSBAND OFFICE
HALT
TO CARLISLE
Loop
MOSSBAND
PLATFORM
N
Mossbandhall
AEY 9/21

XII. A map showing platform positions. Mossband Platform on the left of the main Carlisle to Glasgow road bridge, which was positioned on the down loop and Mossband Office on the up line. (A.E.Young)

42. The Office Halt on the up line facing towards Carlisle is nearing completion on 18th January 1916. (Pearson coll./The Devil's Porridge Museum)

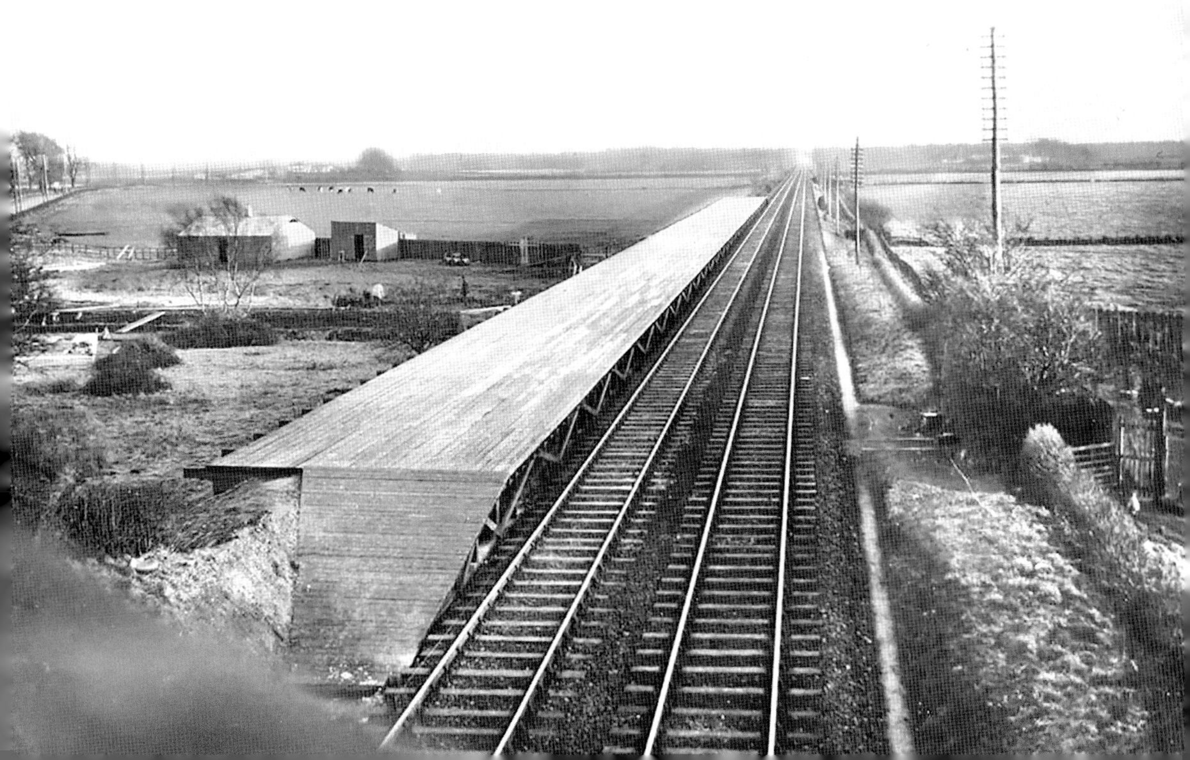

43.   Mossband Platform was located alongside the down loop north of the road bridge. The new signal box can be seen in the middle of the picture alongside the additional sidings provided on the up side. An unidentified CR 0-6-0 is in the sidings, whilst a rake of CR wagons appears to be loaded with building materials for the platform. (Pearson coll./The Devil's Porridge Museum)

Mossband Junction

XIII.   Mossband Junction was opened in 1915 to provide access to the munitions factory at Gretna providing a spur from the south on to the former NBR Gretna branch from Longtown. (A.E. Young)

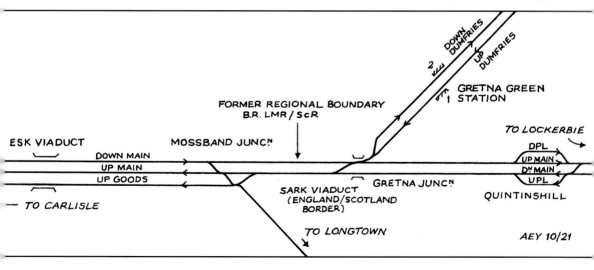

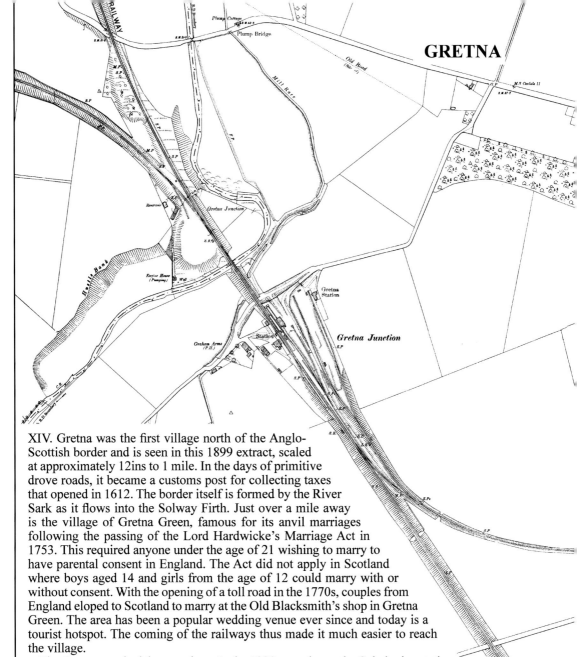

XIV. Gretna was the first village north of the Anglo-Scottish border and is seen in this 1899 extract, scaled at approximately 12ins to 1 mile. In the days of primitive drove roads, it became a customs post for collecting taxes that opened in 1612. The border itself is formed by the River Sark as it flows into the Solway Firth. Just over a mile away is the village of Gretna Green, famous for its anvil marriages following the passing of the Lord Hardwicke's Marriage Act in 1753. This required anyone under the age of 21 wishing to marry to have parental consent in England. The Act did not apply in Scotland where boys aged 14 and girls from the age of 12 could marry with or without consent. With the opening of a toll road in the 1770s, couples from England eloped to Scotland to marry at the Old Blacksmith's shop in Gretna Green. The area has been a popular wedding venue ever since and today is a tourist hotspot. The coming of the railways thus made it much easier to reach the village.

The Gretna area had three stations. In the 1899 map above, the Caledonian station, opened on 10th September 1847, is alongside the North British terminus reached from the Waverley route by a branch line from Longtown. The NBR station opened on 1st November 1861 but closed during World War I in 1915, the line being used for munitions traffic as shown in map XI on the previous page. This station reopened for goods traffic in August 1923 before closing permanently in September 1951. The Caledonian station was renamed Gretna Junction in 1849. This was retained until 1862-63 in *Bradshaw*. The CR had dropped the junction suffix three years earlier. It closed both to passenger and goods traffic on 10th September 1951. The third station at Gretna Green was served by the GSWR, which is at the top of the map on the line heading west from the junction, the station being off the top left-hand corner of the map. The population of Gretna was 2,057 in 1960.

44. The station was viewed in the up direction. The staff had posed for a semi-official photograph. How many of the advertised products, Epps's Cocoa, Venus Soap, Jeyes Fluid and Tennant's Lager, still exist? The NBR station was to the southeast of the Caledonian one seen here. (LOSA)

45. Class 140 also known as the Dunalastair IV class was photographed just leaving Gretna on an Edinburgh to Carlisle train. The goods yard crane is over the bank on the right. The mini signals on the front of the engine indicate that it is a WCML express. (T.H.Gordon-Tidey/J.Alsop coll.)

L. M. & S. R.
CHILD'S TICKET.

THIRD CLASS. Fare 6½d.

G R E T N A
to
CARLISLE

ISSUED SUBJECT TO TH____ ___ITIONS ON BACK HEREOF.

2160

46.   The CR station looking south on 14th May 1936. The wider view includes the down platform and the station signal box. The Gretna Junction signal box was just before the junction and was to the north of Sark viaduct. It was only just in Scotland as the River Sark forms the border between England and Scotland. (H.C.Casserley)

47.   Jubilee class 4-6-0 no. 5623 on a three-coach down train possibly bound for the Dumfries route on 14th May 1936. The locomotive was named *Palestine* seven months later. (H.C.Casserley)

48. This is a view from August 2007 showing the station in residential use looking in the up direction. It was from this station that signalman James Tinsley left to start his shift at Quintinshill signal box one May morning in 1915. (J.Furneval)

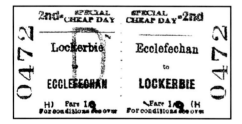

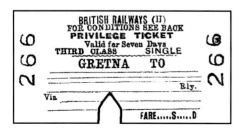

Extract from *Bradshaws Guide*, 1866.

GRETNA.

Telegraph station at Carlisle, 9 miles.

HOTEL.—Gretna Hall.

POST HORSES, FLYS, &c., at the station and hotel. Tariff—1s. 6d. per mile; post boy, 3d. per mile; one horse vehicle, 1s. per mile or 15s. per day; gig, 12s. per day; riding horse, 6s. to 7s. per day; pony, 5s. to 5s. 6d. per day.

MONEY ORDER OFFICE at Carlisle.

The village of Gretna Green, in Dumfries, Scotland, is built on the banks of the Solway Firth, eight miles north of Carlisle. It is the first stage in Scotland from England, and has for more than eighty years been known as the place for the celebration of the marriages of fugitive lovers from England. According to the Scottish law, it was only necessary for a couple to declare before a justice of the peace that they were *unmarried*, and wished to be married, in order to render the ceremony lawful. An Act of parliament has since come into operation which requires a residence in Scotland of too long a duration to suit the purpose of fugitive lovers, and the blacksmith of Gretna Green, like *Othello*, will now find his "occupation gone." More than three hundred marriages took place annually in this and the neighbouring village of Springfield, and the fees varied from one to forty guineas.

Proceeding onward, the line passes the junction of the Dumfries line and Gretna Hall, through Graham's Hill cutting, and opens into a fine view, which about this point presents a most picturesque, varied, and highly romantic appearance.

Gretna Junction

49. The up 'Royal Scot' passes Gretna Junction on 4th June 1960 with Princess Coronation class 4-6-2 no. 46246 *City of Manchester* at its head. The line diverging to the left is the GSWR route to Glasgow via Dumfries and Kilmarnock. (G.W.Morrison)

50. Class 156 DMU no. 156403 comes off the GSWR line from Dumfries on 3rd August 2007. The unit is in Central Trains livery but is on hire to First ScotRail. It later became part of the East Midlands Trains fleet. (J.Furneval)

QUINTINSHILL

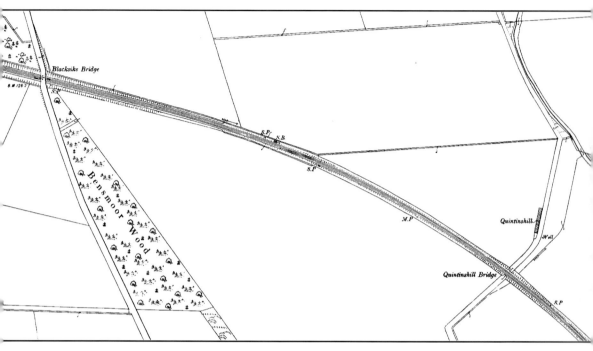

XV.   This 1899 map at 12ins to 1 mile shows the site of the signal box and loops. There was also a siding to serve the rural community. The siding closed on 6th January 1964. We have been unable to trace when it opened but it was temporarily closed on 1st January 1917 during World War I, reopening after the cessation of hostilities.

During the war, Quintinshill was the site of Britain's worst rail disaster on 22nd May 1915, which resulted in 226 deaths and 246 being injured. Both loops were occupied by freight trains and a northbound local train was shunted onto the southbound (up) line to allow a late running sleeping car train to pass. A southbound troop train carrying mainly Territorial soldiers of the 1/7th Leith Battalion of Royal Scots, heading from Larbert to Liverpool where they were due to travel to Gallipoli, was signalled to pass and ploughed into the local train standing on the up line. Within a minute the northbound sleeping car train from London to Glasgow ploughed into the wreckage. Two signalmen (Meakin and Tinsley) were found guilty of culpable homicide (although Tinsley was charged with manslaughter in England, as 27 soldiers died in Carlisle Infirmary, before the case was transferred to Scotland) and both were jailed. Meakin was originally sentenced to three years in Peterhead jail but was released after a year. Both men were re-employed by the Caledonian Railway on release, although not as signalmen.

The deceased soldiers were buried in a mass grave at Rosebank Cemetery, Edinburgh, and a cairn was erected at Quintinshill to mark the centenary of the accident and is located by the site of the disaster. A plaque recording the unfortunate event is located on the pier of the road overbridge.

➔   51.   Two ladies have cycled out to see the wreckage following the Quintinshill crash. The wooden carriages were all lit by Pintsch gas lighting, which resulted in all five trains catching fire with fatal results. The express sleeping car train was double headed by no. 140 of the Dunalastair IV class, seen here, and no. 48 of the 43 Class. Both of the 4-4-0s were eventually repaired.
(Wikipedia/R.Darsley coll.)

➔   52.   The local passenger train was hauled by Cardean class 4-6-0 no. 907. This prestige locomotive was on a running in turn after a works visit. It and the troop train engine 4-4-0 no. 121, a member of the 139 class, were destroyed. The intensity of the fire can be seen in this photograph.
(Wikipedia/R.Darsley coll.)

53. BR Standard 9F class 2-10-0 no. 92233 passes the infamous signal box with a northbound freight. The signalman is keeping a keen eye on it from the signal box window.
(K.A.Gray/
B.McCartney coll.)

54. The inside of the signal box, on 1st July 1972, showing the block instruments, panel and lever frame. Although the box is no more, both loops remain in use.
(G.Kinghorn/
B.McCartney coll.)

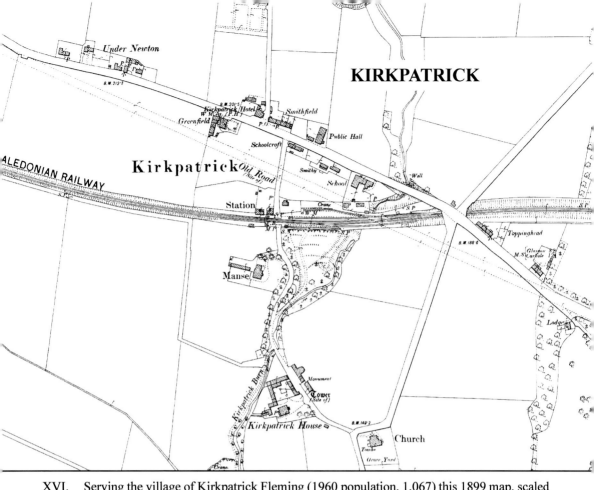

XVI.   Serving the village of Kirkpatrick Fleming (1960 population, 1,067) this 1899 map, scaled at around 18ins to 1 mile, confirms that the station was always known simply as Kirkpatrick. Opened on 10th September 1847, the station closed on 13th June 1960, although it retained its goods facilities until 6th April 1964.

55. This Nicholson & Carter postcard of the station is looking towards Carlisle in around 1910. (J.Alsop coll.)

56.   The photographer was looking towards the north on 28th May 1960. The station is nearing closure but is still smart and tidy. (J.Alsop coll.)

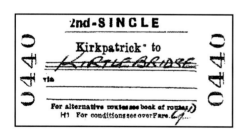

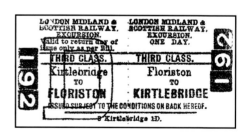

57.   The signal box and the down platform with its shelter, seen on the same day. The signal box was on the south side of the line and east of the road crossing. It was closed in 1971. (N.Forrest/Transport Treasury)

58.   The station is seen here on 23rd May 1960. The LMS carriages formed the 1.50pm Glasgow Central to Carlisle working. The guard walks the platform to close a door left open by a departing passenger. (W.A.C.Smith/Transport Treasury)

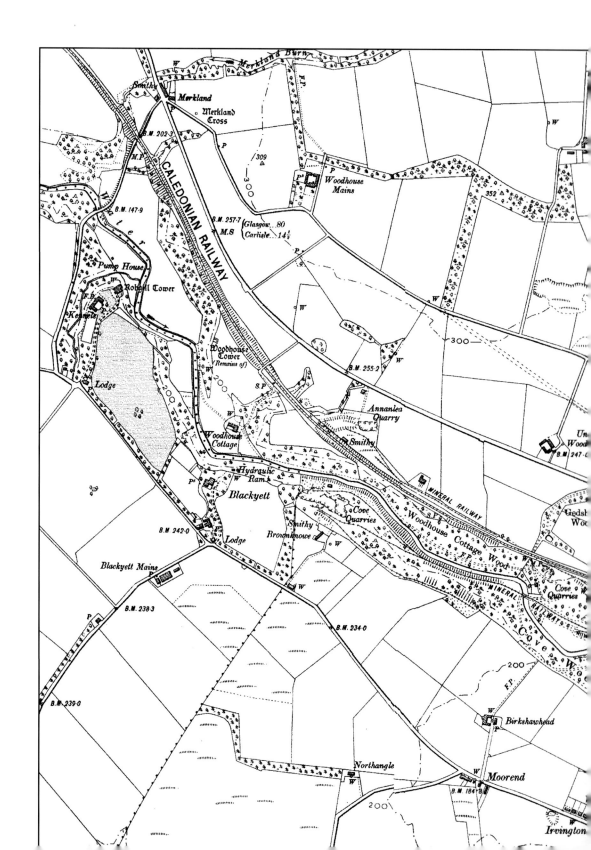

Annanlea & Cove Quarries

XVII. Seen here in 1899, scaled at 4ins to 1 mile, Annanlea and Cove quarries were located north of Kirkpatrick. Quarrying of Sandstone was first recorded as taking place as early as 1794. Whilst used locally for paving, steps and gravestones, as transport improved its output was later moved further afield. The two quarries were connected to the Caledonian line by the 1850s. After a period of closure, a new company, New Cove Quarries, was formed in 1895 to take the lease of Cove Quarries on the estate of the Greville-Nugent family, which produced both red and white sandstone. The quarries were described as follows:

'The extent of the quarry ground is nearly a mile in length, by the side of the River Kirtle. The white stone from here, lying on the east side of the river, was the material with which Eden Bridges was built at a cost of £80,000... the red stone on the west side... was chiefly worked by the late Mr Thomas Nelson, contractor, for Silloth Dock and Railway and many other large works which he had in hand. The present works will be connected by a siding from the Caledonian main line, worked by a small locomotive engine, and a railway laid to connect both sides of the river...'

Although the quarry had previously been worked in connection with railway construction it seems that there had been no rail connection into the quarry; presumably, a loading facility had been provided adjacent to the main line.

The new rail system was quite extensive and when it became operational a new standard gauge 0-4-0 tank locomotive was purchased from Andrew Barclay of Kilmarnock in 1897. It was advertised for sale in October 1904 and a new slightly larger 0-4-0 tank locomotive was then purchased, also from Andrew Barclay. A second-hand 0-4-0 tank locomotive built by Fletcher Jennings at Whitehaven was also acquired in 1898 following rebuilding by Andrew Barclay and a second-hand 0-6-0 tank loco by Hudswell Clarke is said to have worked there for a brief period just prior to closure.

The company went into liquidation in December 1907 but a new company, Cove Quarries Ltd, was formed in 1909 and the quarries continued to work until 1912; this company went into liquidation in 1913. The quarries were offered for letting in April 1914 but were then out of use and the track was lifted.

Some quarrying is still undertaken at Cove today, but the rail links have long since disappeared.

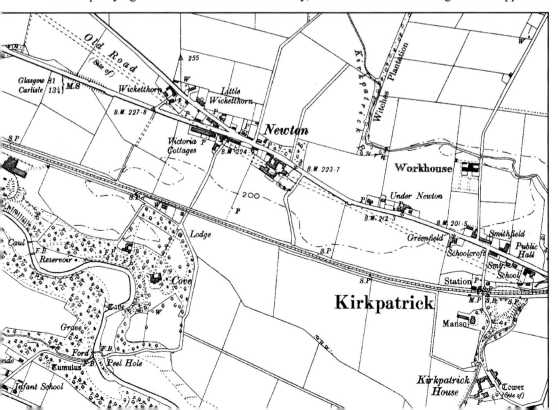

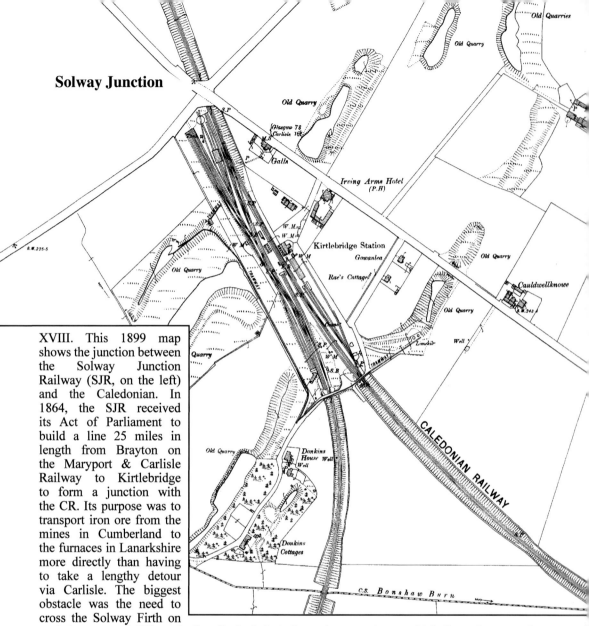

Solway Junction

XVIII. This 1899 map shows the junction between the Solway Junction Railway (SJR, on the left) and the Caledonian. In 1864, the SJR received its Act of Parliament to build a line 25 miles in length from Brayton on the Maryport & Carlisle Railway to Kirtlebridge to form a junction with the CR. Its purpose was to transport iron ore from the mines in Cumberland to the furnaces in Lanarkshire more directly than having to take a lengthy detour via Carlisle. The biggest obstacle was the need to cross the Solway Firth on a viaduct some 2,554 yards (1 mile 8 chains) from shore to shore, which formed yet another border crossing between England with Scotland and linking Bowness-on-Solway with Annan in Dumfriesshire. Construction of the viaduct was the biggest challenge requiring considerable piling at low tide. It took over three years to complete and comprised wrought iron piers

The northern section from Annan (later Annan Shawhill station) to Kirtlebridge was the first to open on 13th September 1869 with the entire line opening on 8th August 1870 when the passenger service was introduced. However, not long after it opened, the iron ore traffic declined as imported ore was cheaper. In January 1881, the pillars were severely damaged by frost due to water ingress and then freezing, cracking the columns. As a result, the viaduct was closed until 1884 while the company raised the necessary funds to strengthen it. The Caledonian was a major shareholder in the SJR company and in 1895 it was taken over by them.

Traffic over the line greatly increased during World War I but by 1921 the viaduct required considerable repairs and it was uneconomical to authorise them. The line was immediately closed south of Annan both to passenger and goods in May 1921, services continuing between Annan and Kirtlebridge until 27th April 1931 when the line was closed to all traffic.

59.   With Kirtlebridge station and signal box in the distance, the Solway line came in from the left with the limestone narrow gauge lines and shed in the foreground. The main line is on the right. (Fleetwood Shaw/E.Breck coll.)

60. 4-4-0T no. 15027 was on the 10.47am train from Kirtlebridge. The train is heading to Annan Shawhill in the last year of operation. After most of the line closed in 1921, the section of the branch between Annan and Kirtlebridge closed 10 years later, on 27th April 1931. (E.Breck coll.)

KIRTLEBRIDGE

61. Bradshaw referred to the station as 'Kirtlebridge for Eaglesfield' until 1955, although the station appeared elsewhere as Kirtlebridge. The first station opened in February 1848 but was relocated a mile to the north by October 1869. The 1899 map on the previous page shows a complex of narrow gauge lines, which served the limestone quarries around Kirtlebridge. Opened in the 18th century, by 1900, only one, Donkins, to the east of the main line, remained in business. A line linking quarry sites either side of the Caledonian crossed it on a bridge.

On 2nd October 1872, the 9pm 'Special Scotch Mail' train travelling north from London Euston with coaches for Edinburgh, Glasgow, Perth and Aberdeen, collided with a freight train which was being shunted, with wagons being left on the down main line. Eleven people were killed, including the driver of the express, and 15 injured when the express hit the static wagons at some 40mph. With the line blocked for a day, trains were diverted over the GSWR between Carlisle and Dumfries before taking the Lockerbie line, where they could regain their intended route. The inquest found that there was no method of safe working.

The station and signal box shown above were photographed on 28th May 1960, less than a month before closure, which took place on 13th June of that year. The far side of the island platform was used for the Solway Junction line. Closure to goods traffic followed on 6th April 1964. (N.Forrest/Transport Treasury)

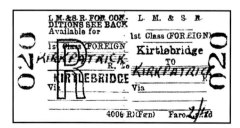

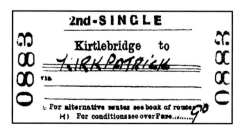

62.   A view of the station in the up direction. The station running-in board reads 'Kirtlebridge for Eaglesfield and Middlebie'. Eaglesfield is a linear village about a mile north and now separated by Junction 20 of the M74 Motorway. Middlebie was a further 1½ miles further north. (LOSA)

63.   Taken on the same day as picture 61, this picture shows the up platform and the gardening skills of the station staff. They have made effective use of the goods shed wall to support the climbing plants. (N.Forrest/Transport Treasury)

64. Clan class 4-6-2 no. 72008 *Clan MacLeod* was passing the station and goods yard on 4th June 1960 with a Perth to London Euston train. Besides the crane, the roof of the goods shed behind the coaches can be seen. BR Standard class no. 72008 was a Carlisle-based locomotive, built at Crewe in 1952 and withdrawn in April 1966. The class were not noted for their sparkling performances and were the equivalent of a 'Black 5' with a' bit in hand'! (G.W.Morrison)

Kirtlebridge Engine Shed

65. The engine shed was situated to the north of the station, as shown on map XVIII (opposite picture 59). Opened with the SJR in September 1869, the original shed was demolished in July 1895 and replaced by a new timber one which could hold two locomotives under cover. The shed closed with the withdrawal of passenger and freight services to Annan on 25th April 1931. Unfortunately, on 20th June 1936, the doors remained closed.
(W.A.Camwell/Stephenson Locomotive Society coll.)

ECCLEFECHAN.

Telegraph station at Lockerbie, 5½ miles.
HOTEL.—Bush.
FAIRS.—Once a month.

The town of Ecclefechan is remarkable for nothing but its frequent and well-attended markets and fairs. From the station may be perceived a strong square keep or tower, the seat of General Matthew Sharpe, and known as *Hoddam Castle*, formerly a place of considerable importance as a border stronghold, and at present distinguished as one of the most delightful residences in Dumfriesshire. Opposite the castle, on a conspicuous mount, stands *Trailtron*, known as the Tower of Repentance, and formerly used as a beacon. It is said that Sir Richard Steele, while residing near this place, saw a shepherd boy reading his Bible, and asked him what he learned from it? "The way to heaven," answered the boy. "And can you show it to me?" said Sir Richard, in banter. "You must go by that tower," replied the shepherd, and he pointed to the Tower of Repentance.

Extract from *Bradshaws Guide*, 1866.

ECCLEFECHAN

66.　A view of the station's up platform on 28th May 1960. The main building was a compact version of the Scottish baronial style. (N.Forrest/Transport Treasury)

XIX.　Seen here in 1899, the station opened with the line on 10th September 1847. It closed to passengers on 13th June 1960 when the population of the village was 611. It remained open for goods traffic until 28th October 1963.

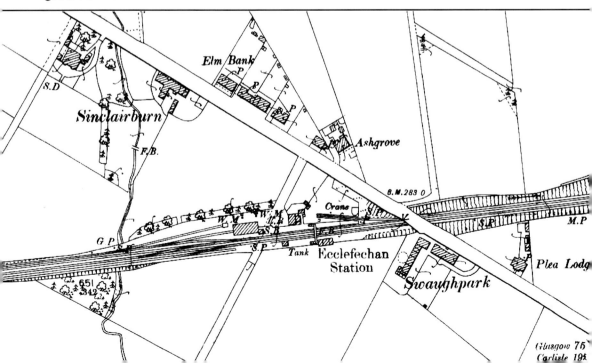

67. The photograph of the footbridge with a view of the down platform was taken in the 1950s. (LOSA)

68. By the time this photograph was taken on 28th May 1960, the focus of the photograph was the signal box and goods shed. (N.Forrest/Transport Treasury)

Castlemilk Goods

XX. Although no opening date for the goods station at Castlemilk has been traced, the facilities were in use on this 1899 map (approximately 12ins to 1 mile) serving the large estate located three miles south of Lockerbie. The baronial mansion was built between 1864 and 1870 on the site of a former building, which was constructed in 1796. Castlemilk Goods was closed temporarily on 1st January 1917 during World War I and subsequently reopened. It closed permanently on 6th April 1964.

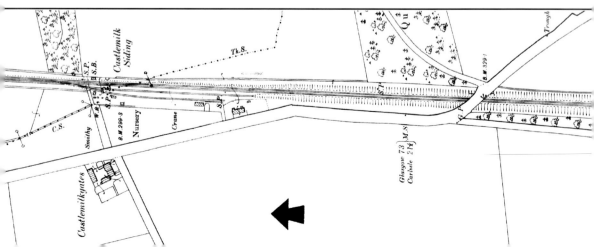

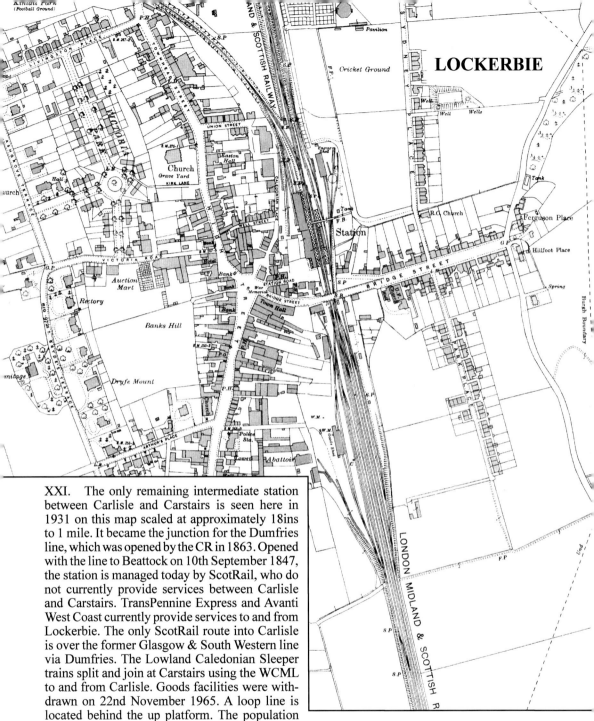

LOCKERBIE

XXI. The only remaining intermediate station between Carlisle and Carstairs is seen here in 1931 on this map scaled at approximately 18ins to 1 mile. It became the junction for the Dumfries line, which was opened by the CR in 1863. Opened with the line to Beattock on 10th September 1847, the station is managed today by ScotRail, who do not currently provide services between Carlisle and Carstairs. TransPennine Express and Avanti West Coast currently provide services to and from Lockerbie. The only ScotRail route into Carlisle is over the former Glasgow & South Western line via Dumfries. The Lowland Caledonian Sleeper trains split and join at Carstairs using the WCML to and from Carlisle. Goods facilities were withdrawn on 22nd November 1965. A loop line is located behind the up platform. The population in 2011 was 4,287, with the station handling 272,800 passengers in 2018-19.

The town achieved distressing international publicity when a terrorist attack resulted in the destruction of Pan Am Flight 103 travelling between Frankfurt and Detroit on 21st December 1988. Having made a scheduled stop at London Heathrow and bound for another at New York, it exploded over the town following the detonating of a bomb killing all 259 people on board. This also resulted in debris from the plane killing a further 11 residents and resulting in the destruction of several houses in Sherwood Crescent, 21 of which were subsequently demolished.

69.　The staff are posed for this picture of the station from the road bridge. The locomotive is Dunalastair class 4-4-0 no. 966 and the miniature signal arms on the chimney indicate that this is an Edinburgh to Carlisle working via Carstairs. The running-in board indicates that this is the junction for Dumfries and Portpatrick, the latter involving a long journey through GSWR territory to reach it. (LOSA)

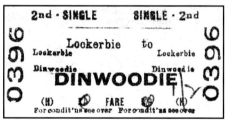

70.　The 4-4-0 is at the northern end of the up platform, with the goods yard behind the train. The 'Dunalastair' series of locomotives, built by J.F.McIntosh were renowned for speed and feats of haulage. They became the standard CR express passenger locomotive. (R.M.Casserley coll.)

71. On 13th June 1959, the Stephenson Locomotive Society (SLS) Golden Jubilee was in Lockerbie about to take the branch to Dumfries. The locomotive was a 4-4-0 Great North of Scotland F class no. 49 *Gordon Highlander*. This carried BR no. 62277 and was part of the LNER's D40 class. No. 49 was one of several 'reserved' locomotives that were repainted into former liveries and worked excursion trains for some years before being retired to the Glasgow Museum of Transport. It is currently on loan to the Scottish Railway Preservation Centre at Bo'ness. The CR 0-4-4T station pilot is behind the fence. (W.A.C.Smith/Transport Treasury)

72. Class 185 DMU no. 185120 is on a TransPennine Express service to Manchester Airport. This unit was built by Siemens in 2005 and is one of the UK versions of their 'Desiro' type. They have Cummins diesel engines and Voith transmission with a top speed of 100 mph. The fully accessible footbridge with lifts can be seen in the background. (B.E.Morrison)

73.   Virgin Trains class 220 Voyager no. 220015 was named *Solway Voyager* here, on 28th August 2002, when it ran as a special train conveying press and invited guests from Carlisle to Edinburgh and back. The clock tower of the town hall can be seen on the right. (D.A.Lovett)

➜   Extract from *Bradshaws Guide*, 1866.

74.   The roadside view of the main station buildings was photographed on 1st June 2021. The distinctive style is impressive but not overbearing. The former station master's flat is now the home of Dumfries & District Model Railway Club. (D.A.Lovett)

LOCKERBIE.

A telegraph station.

HOTEL.—George.

MARKET DAY.—Thursday.

FAIRS.—Second Thursday in January, February, March, and May, *o. s.*; Thursday in week before April 23rd; June 3rd Thursday, *o.s.*; August 13th, or Tuesday after; Thursday in week before 30th September; October, 2nd Thursday after Falkirk; Thursday in week after 1st Wednesday in November.

Looking north from this station, there being no curve, we can see down the line a very long way. Here "Old Mortality" died at Brick Hall, in 1801. *Lockerbie Hall*, J. Douglas, Esq., and *Mains Tower*, which belonged to the Johnstones, are close at hand.

Lockerbie Engine Shed

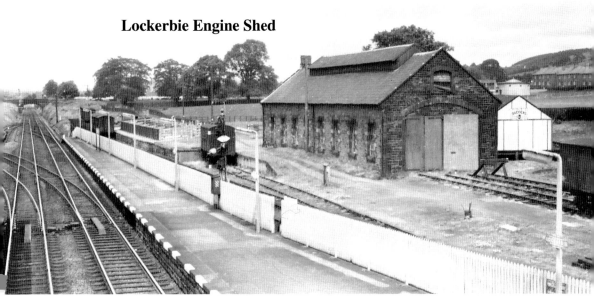

75.   Map XXI (opposite picture 68) shows the facilities that existed north of the station at the two-road shed when it closed in April 1931, although it remained as a stabling and a footplate crew signing-on point until 5th February 1951. A sub-shed of Beattock; footplate staff were transferred to the mother shed on closure of Lockerbie. Dumfries branch trains were worked from the LMS shed at Dumfries following Grouping in 1923.

   Opened in 1863 to coincide with the opening of the Dumfries branch, it had a 42ft turntable that was transferred to Beattock on closure. The shed building survived until 1985 when it was finally demolished. The photo looks north on 19th June 1961 with the shed on the right. The junction for the line to Dumfries is on the left. The platform edging is unusual and is normally a continuous painted line. (R.S.Carpenter)

76.   Outside the shed in June 1959 was 0-4-4T no. 55260. Originally CR 439 class design, this locomotive was one of 10 built after the grouping in 1925 by the LMS who rated it 2P in its power classification scheme. (N.Forrest/Transport Treasury)

DUMFRIES BRANCH FROM LOCKERBIE

Dumfries Branch Junction

We leave Lockerbie to follow the Caledonian line to Dumfries. This was another attempt by the CR to 'occupy the space' on the map rather than be profitable.

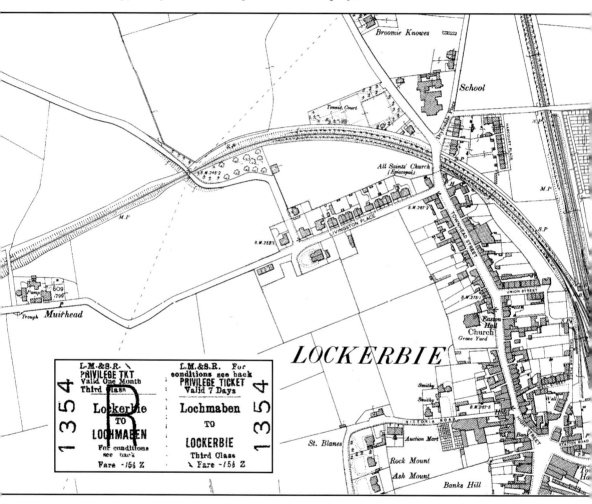

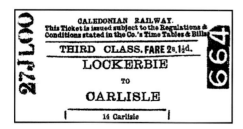

XXII. The CR opened its branch line from Lockerbie to Dumfries on 1st September 1863 as seen here on this 1899 map, scaled at approximately 12ins to 1 mile. The Caledonian had wanted to open its own station at Dumfries St Mary's but was forced by the GSWR to terminate at their station. The St Mary's site became the Caledonian Goods Station and housed the engine shed. The branch lost its passenger services on 19th May 1952 and closed completely in 1966 following the withdrawal of goods traffic.

LOCHMABEN

XXIII. Seen here in 1899, the station opened with the line on 1st September 1863. Although passenger services were withdrawn on 19th May 1952, goods traffic was retained until 4th May 1964, two years before the line closed. The population in 2011 was 1,942. The map is scaled at 12ins to 1 mile.

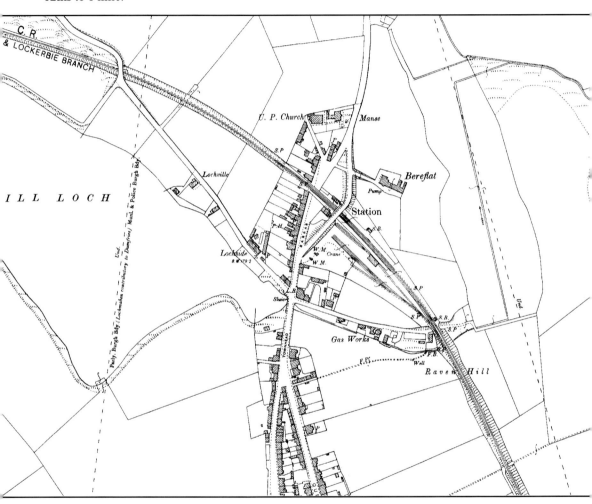

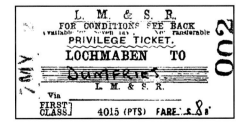

LOCHMABEN,

A telegraph station, and place at which the tourist would do well to make a temporary sojourn. It is poetically called the "Queen of the Lochs," from its situation amid so many sheets of water.

From hence the line continues its course through SHIELDHILL, AMISFIELD, and LOCHARBRIGGS to DUMFRIES, where it becomes connected with the Castle Douglas line.

Extract from *Bradshaws Guide*, 1866.

77. The railway here was double track with two platforms. The line was singled before closure with passing loops in stations only. (LOSA)

78. The station after closure was a dismal sight. The down platform, shelter and signal box have gone, and the station house is boarded up. As in picture 77, we are looking south. (N.Forrest/Transport Treasury)

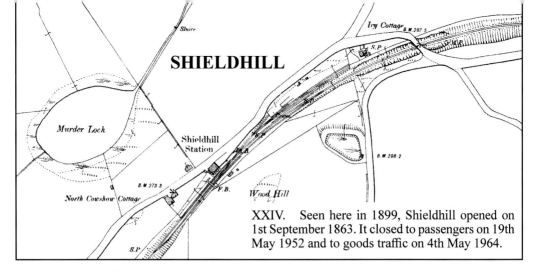

SHIELDHILL

XXIV. Seen here in 1899, Shieldhill opened on 1st September 1863. It closed to passengers on 19th May 1952 and to goods traffic on 4th May 1964.

79. Despite their simplicity, the stations on the line added something to the landscape, unlike the metal and glass shelters on new stations today. Both here and at Lochmaben there were more than adequate freight facilities. (LOSA)

80. This was the state of the station in December 1957. The single track was worked on the 'one engine in steam' principle. (N.Forrest/Transport Treasury)

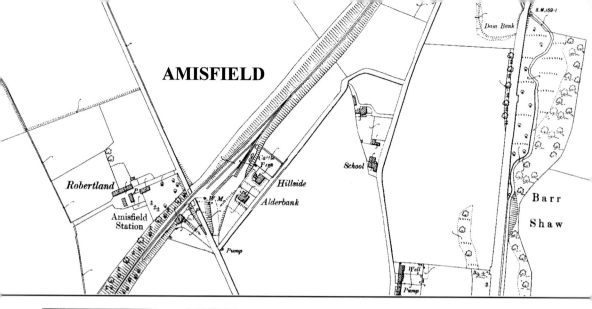

AMISFIELD

81. There was a design continuity between the different stations though Amisfield was not a passing point and had just a single track in passenger days. (LOSA)

82. The station closed in 1952 and this was its state on 14th July 1968 after the track had been lifted. Amisfield Town consisted of three scattered terraces. (J.Alsop)

← XXV.   Seen here in 1899, Amisfield opened on 1st September 1863. It closed to passengers on 19th May 1952 and to goods traffic on 4th May 1964. This extract is scaled at 18ins to 1 mile.

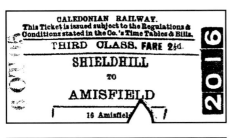

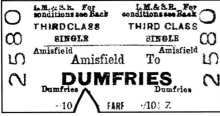

Knowehead Quarry, Locharbriggs

XXVI.   The quarry here was opened in 1890 by W.G.Patterson & Co. who quarried a distinctive red sandstone, used on buildings in Dumfries, Edinburgh and Glasgow, although it was also exported elsewhere. The steps of the Statue of Liberty in New York were built using stone from the quarry, which is seen here on this 1900 extract, scaled at approximately 12ins to 1 mile.

The Ballochmyle brickworks, which was a subsidiary company of the quarry owners, opened here in 1935. It used the residue from the quarry operations, which was mixed with lime and then pressed into moulds before being baked in a large oven. The brickworks employed around a dozen and closed in 1977.

The quarry closed in 1974 and part of the site is now used by an auto salvage company.

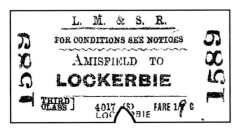

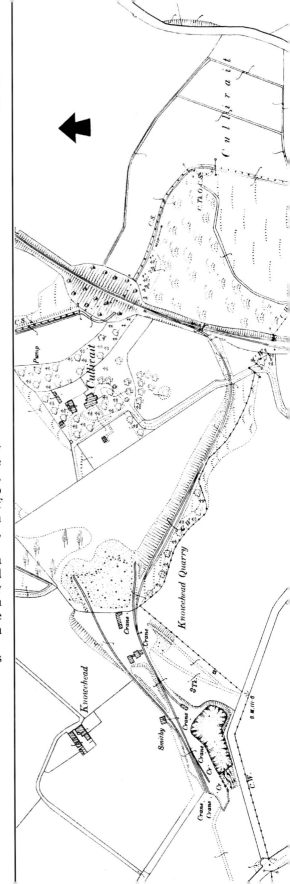

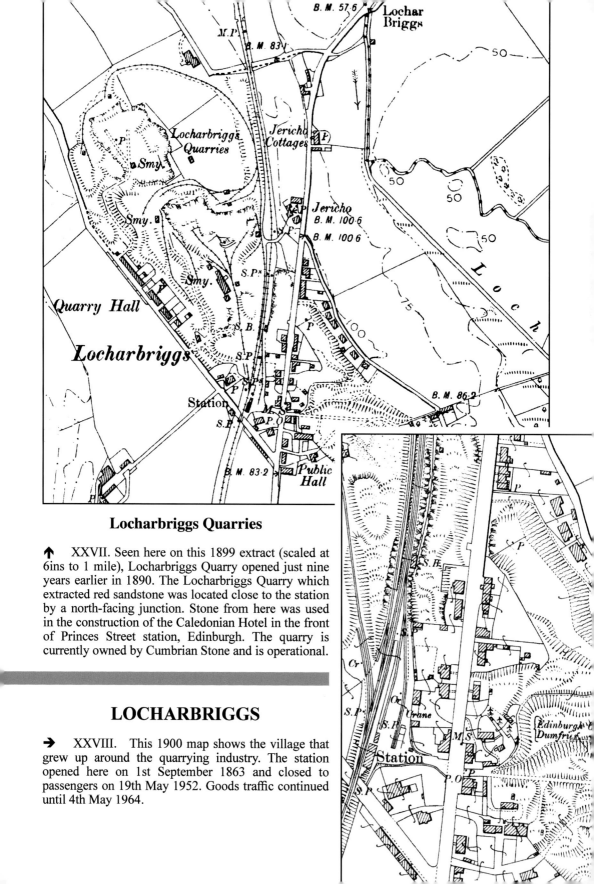

Locharbriggs Quarries

⬆ XXVII. Seen here on this 1899 extract (scaled at 6ins to 1 mile), Locharbriggs Quarry opened just nine years earlier in 1890. The Locharbriggs Quarry which extracted red sandstone was located close to the station by a north-facing junction. Stone from here was used in the construction of the Caledonian Hotel in the front of Princes Street station, Edinburgh. The quarry is currently owned by Cumbrian Stone and is operational.

LOCHARBRIGGS

➔ XXVIII. This 1900 map shows the village that grew up around the quarrying industry. The station opened here on 1st September 1863 and closed to passengers on 19th May 1952. Goods traffic continued until 4th May 1964.

83.   The station buildings were on the single platform but there were considerable sidings for the surrounding quarries. (LOSA)

84.   Activity here shows that the quarries did generate some traffic for the line. Near the impressive signal box is a gleaming CR 0-6-0 with mineral wagons. There is an impressive contraption on the chimney of the building just left of the signal box. The telegraph poles on this line are notable too as they all seem to be double poles. (LOSA)

HEATHHALL HALT

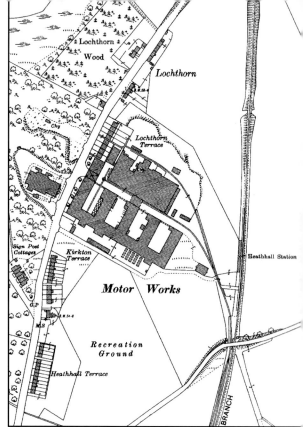

XXIX.   Seen here on this 1931 map (scaled at approximately 12ins to 1 mile) are the works of the old Arrol Motor Car Company and its adjacent halt for factory workers.

Former locomotive engineer, George Johnston, trained at Neilson, Reid & Co at Springburn, Glasgow. After a brief experiment with producing a steam tram for Glasgow Corporation Tramways, he turned his interests to the fledgling motor car industry. He received backing from Sir William Arrol MP, the famous Scottish Engineer, whose company included the building of the Forth and Tay Bridges (the replacement for Bouch's collapsed structure) and Tower Bridge in London amongst its impressive portfolio.

Initially, cars, the first to be built in the UK, were produced by the Mo-Car Syndicate in the east end of Glasgow. When it was destroyed by fire in 1901 the company moved to Paisley.

The company purchased land north of Dumfries at Heathhall, adjacent to the branch from Lockerbie. Here a new factory was built using reinforced concrete and large expanses of glass to provide plenty of natural light. It was the first structure of this type to be built in the UK. It was modelled on car plants in Detroit, USA, where Packhard and Ford both had modern factories. The Heathhall facility was built in an E shape and opened in July 1913. It was extended by the addition of two further wings during 1916.

A platform was provided to bring in workers although it did not appear in public timetables. Sidings were provided at the site to bring in raw materials and for the delivery of finished vehicles.

Car production continued at Heathhall until the late 1920s before finally closing in 1931. During World War II (1939-45) the factory was used to construct aircraft, which were then taken to nearby RAF Dumfries for onward delivery to other wartime airfields.

Post-war, the North British Rubber Company acquired the site in 1946 and, over the years, items produced included Wellington boots, shoes, golf balls, bathing caps, flooring and conveyor belts. The factory closed in 2013 and is currently derelict. It has Listed status and there are hopes that it may still have a future of some sort.

85.   This is an aerial view of the Arrol-Aster car factory. In the left background is the platform of the halt. A goods line to the factory comes from the branch and generates at least three sidings in the factory perimeter. (RCAHMS/Dumfries Museum)

86.   The factory gateway was designed to impress. (Courtesy of Dumfries Museum)

87.   A view into the factory along one of the sidings where setts are being laid. An overhead crane spans the track. (Courtesy of Dumfries Museum)

88.   Another sidings view shows railway wagons, though more likely these contained materials for the contractors building the extension under construction. (Courtesy of Dumfries Museum)

Approaching Dumfries

89.   The four-day SLS/BLS (Branch Line Society) 'Scottish Rambler No. 2' was approaching Dumfries from the Lockerbie branch on 15th April 1963, hauled by Jubilee class 4-6-0 no. 45588 *Kashmir*. This locomotive entered traffic on 15th December 1934. *Kashmir* spent 20 years at Blackpool before being transferred to Carlisle Upperby. It moved to Kingmoor in July 1962 and was withdrawn in May 1965. It was one of the members of the class built by the North British Locomotive Co Ltd at their Queens Park Works in Glasgow. (K.A.Gray/B.McCartney coll.)

Dumfries (Caledonian) Engine Shed

XXX.   This 1900 map shows the CR engine shed at St. Mary's. Opened in August 1863 it has a 42ft turntable installed in 1902. Following the Grouping in 1923, when the London, Midland & Scottish Railway (LMS) took over both the CR and the GSWR, it eventually allowed the Caledonian shed to be closed with staff and locomotives moving to the former GSWR shed with St Mary's shed being used as a Carriage & Wagon Works until the 1960s.

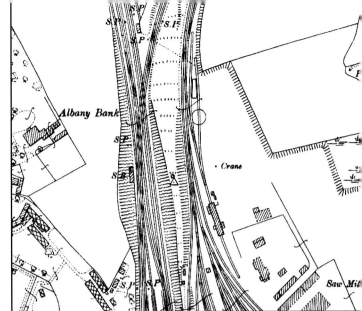

90.   The CR shed at St. Mary's Dumfries was closed on 20th June 1936, leaving just an external view available to the photographer. (W.A.Camwell/Stephenson Locomotive Society coll.)

91.   The engine shed, seen on 21st September 1965, was at the apex of a fan of sidings leading to the goods yard and interchange with the GSWR. (R.S.Carpenter)

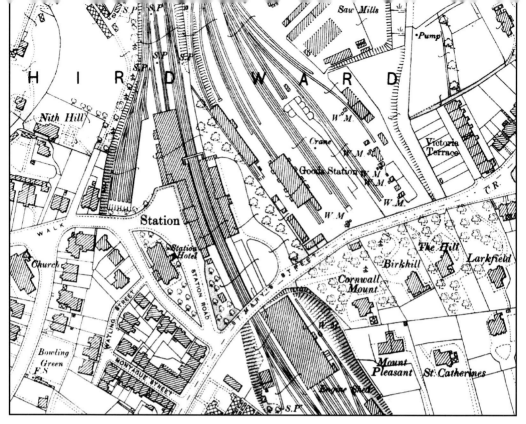

Dumfries St Mary's Goods

XXXI. Originally intended as the terminus of the line before the GSWR objected and insisted on the line terminating at their own station adjacent, it was used as a goods yard. Seen here in 1900, it opened with the line in 1863 and closed on 17th Oct 1966. The large goods shed survives as part of an industrial estate.

92. The CR goods shed at St Mary's was, by 8th June 2021, the only part of the Caledonian buildings to survive. It was being used by a firm of decorators in what is now St. Mary's industrial estate. (D.A.Lovett)

DUMFRIES (GSWR STATION)

XXXII.   This 1900 extract is scaled at approximately 4ins to 1 mile. Dumfries has grown over the years. In 1960 it had a population of 27,430 which had grown to 39,520 50 years later, when the 2011 census was carried out. The station was opened by the Glasgow, Dumfries & Carlisle Railway on 23rd August 1848 and served as a temporary terminus for trains to and from Carlisle. In 1849 the permanent station opened following extension of the line northwards and on 28th October 1850 the line became part of the GSWR, which had been formed by amalgamating several smaller companies. The current station, located 15 chains north, opened on 13th September 1859 with the opening of the line to Castle Douglas that was extended to Stranraer in 1861 and was known as the Port Road. After the opening of the Lockerbie branch in 1863, the final line to open was the Cairn Valley branch to Moniaive in 1905.

Although it was the last to be built, the Moniaive line closed completely in 1949. The Lockerbie line lost its passenger services in 1952 and goods traffic ceased in 1966. The Port Road to Stranraer closed to all traffic in 1965, save for the short section at the Dumfries end that served an oil depot at Maxwelltown until 1994.

Dumfries station is served today by ScotRail services from Carlisle to Glasgow Central. The line through Dumfries is also used for diversions and for freight traffic. A train crew depot was established at the station in 2002.

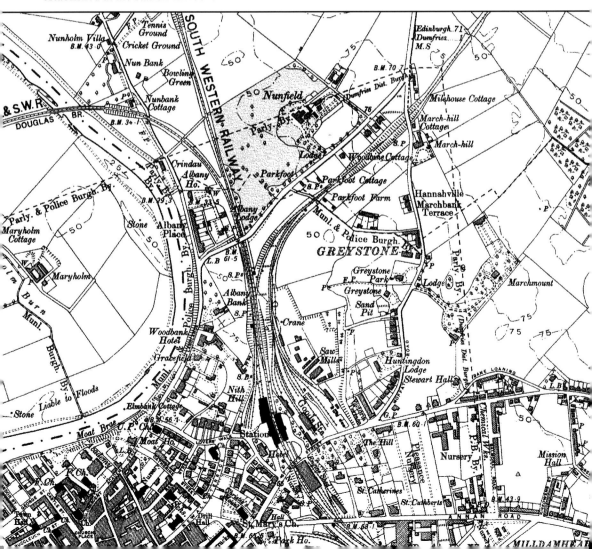

93.   The GSWR ensured that the CR did not build its own station and that it used their own. This is an R.Grieve postcard from around 1910 with the station viewed north to west from the bridge. (J.Alsop coll.)

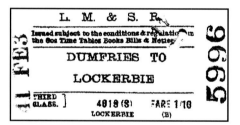

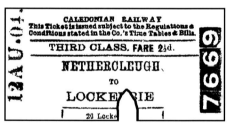

94.   CR 4-6-0 no. 17911 in LMS livery is about to leave Dumfries for Carlisle. The 184 class were mixed traffic locomotives built by McIntosh and were those that he designed before retirement. They were the most successful of his 4-6-0 designs. Built in December 1914, no. 17911 survived until April 1935. (Milepost 92½/Transport Treasury)

95. 0-6-0 no. 57602 was one of the CR class 812s designed by McIntosh in 1899. This view is looking north, and this is an up express from Glasgow to Stranraer. It is about to return north to take the Stranraer line with banking assistance from no. 57602, seen here at the rear of the train. (B.Brooksbank/Geograph)

96. Class 47 Co-Co DE no. 47535 calls with the 10.35 Stranraer Harbour to London Euston on 9th June 1983. This had travelled over the Ayr – Kilmarnock line as the former GSWR Port Road, the direct line between Dumfries and Stranraer, had been closed in June 1965. (G.W.Morrison)

97.　On 8th June 2021, class 156 DMUs nos 156509 and 156503, in Saltire livery, were on a Glasgow Central to Newcastle Central via Carlisle working. The Saltire livery was devised in September 2008 and, with the ScotRail brand, is owned by Transport Scotland. The station gardens here are maintained by volunteers and include a double-headed barrel-train planter. (D.A.Lovett)

98.　This is an external view of the station taken on 8th June 2021. The Italianate-style building was listed in 1997 and the listing includes the platforms, lamp standards, signal box, chargeman's hut, gates and railings. (D.A.Lovett)

Dumfries GSWR Engine Shed

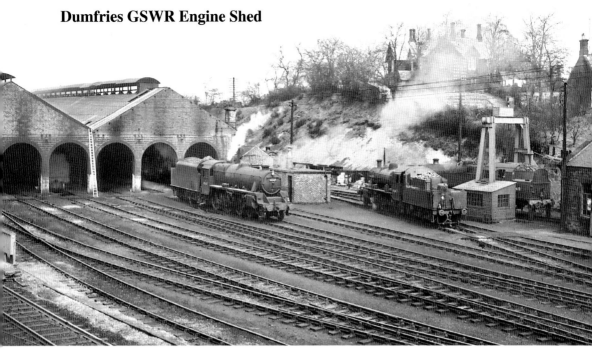

99. A general view of the shed at Easter 1966 has a 4-6-0 no. 45162 and 2-6-0 no. 46478 awaiting their next duties. The first is a 'Black 5' mixed traffic loco and the second an LMS Ivatt design, built by BR in the former LNER Darlington Works. (Milepost 92½/Transport Treasury)

100.   No. 55124 0-4-4T was inside the shed on 12th May 1957. This CR 19 class locomotive was built in May 1895 and was withdrawn from Dalry Road Shed, Edinburgh, on 30th September 1961 and was the last of the class to be withdrawn. (G.W.Morrison)

NETHERCLEUGH

We now return to the West Coast Main Line joining at the next station north of Lockerbie.

XXXIII. Seen here in 1899, Nethercleugh opened with the line on 10th September 1847. It was closed both to goods and passenger services on 13th June 1960.

101. *(below)* The station looking south from the up platform with the level crossing and signal cabin in view. It served the rural area around Nethercleugh and the estate at Jardine Hall. (LOSA)

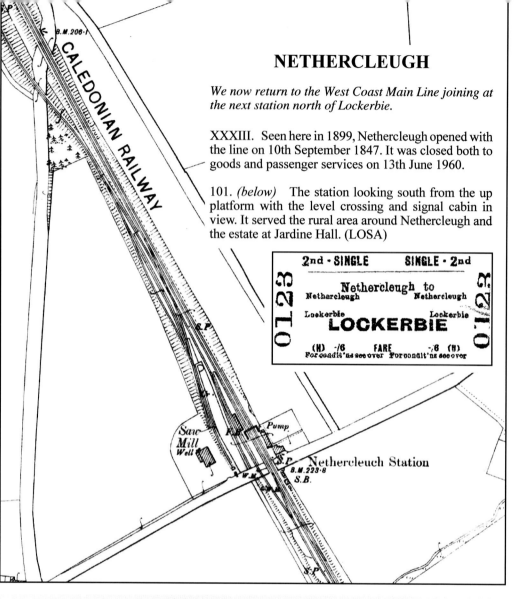

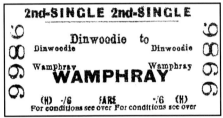

102. The station and signal box from the other direction on 28th May 1960. The level crossing was removed upon electrification, and little remains apart from a railway cottage. (N.Forrest/Transport Treasury)

DINWOODIE

XXXIV. This extract is also dated 1899. *Bradshaw* first recorded the station as coming into use in May 1853. It closed both to passenger and goods traffic on 13th June 1960.

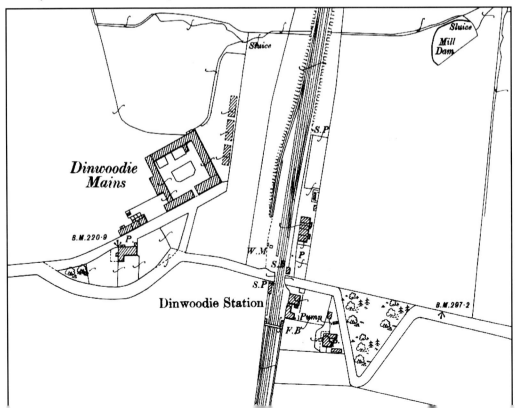

103.	The station and signal box are seen on 28th May 1960. There was a rear-end collision here on 25th October 1928, the derailment causing some of the train to slide down the embankment. (N.Forrest/Transport Treasury)

104.	The station house with its clock is rather attractive. Again, the date is 28th May 1960. It is now a private dwelling; the level crossing having been replaced by a road overbridge. (N.Forrest/Transport Treasury)

105.	Class 92 Co-Co WE no. 92017 *Bart the Engine*, in Stobart Rail livery, was on a southbound ballast train on 20th May 2011, near the former site of Dinwoodie station. (B.McCartney)

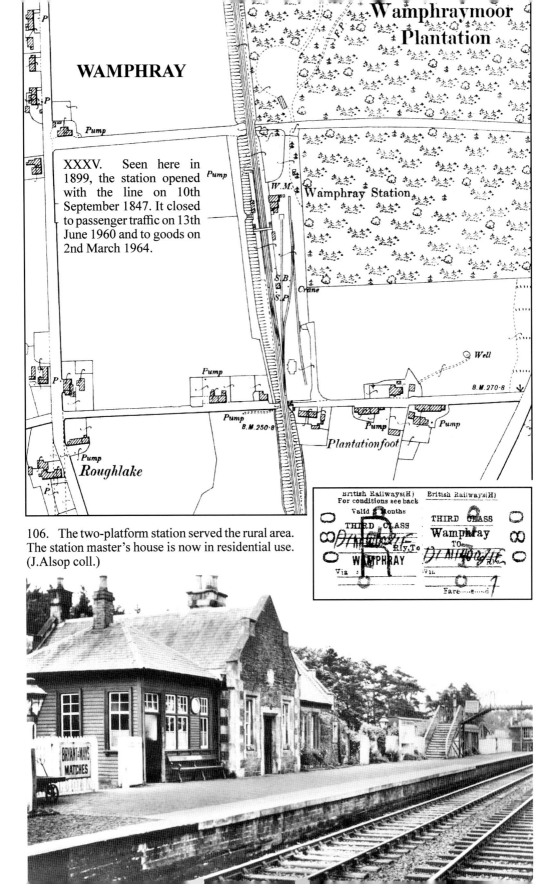

WAMPHRAY

Wamphraymoor Plantation

XXXV. Seen here in 1899, the station opened with the line on 10th September 1847. It closed to passenger traffic on 13th June 1960 and to goods on 2nd March 1964.

Pump

Pump

W.M.

Wamphray Station

S.B.
S.P.

Crane

Well

B.M.270·8

Pump

Pump
B.M.250·8

Plantationfoot

Pump

Pump

Pump

Roughlake

106. The two-platform station served the rural area. The station master's house is now in residential use. (J.Alsop coll.)

British Railways(H)   British Railways(H)
For conditions see back
Valid 3 months
THIRD CLASS   THIRD CLASS
DALMAHOYIE   Wamphray
Rly To   TO
WAMPHRAY   DALMAHOYIE
Via   Via
Fare

BRYANT-MAYS
MATCHES

107.   The station buildings became redundant in 1960 and were located on the southbound up platform. The local area is known as Newtown and the station was informally called Newtown Wamphray. An underbridge now marks the spot of the former station. (LOSA)

BEATTOCK

108.   Midland Railway compound 4-4-0 no. 901 enters the station with a Manchester Victoria to Edinburgh train on 1st August 1931. Note the sign 'change for Moffat' on the running-in board. The Moffat branch will feature in a future *Beattock to Carstairs* album. (H.C.Casserley)

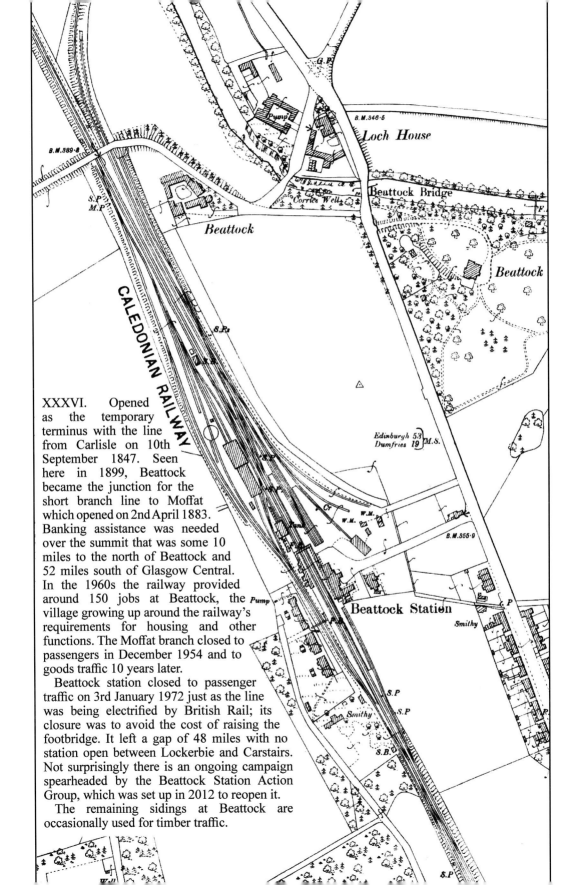

XXXVI. Opened as the temporary terminus with the line from Carlisle on 10th September 1847. Seen here in 1899, Beattock became the junction for the short branch line to Moffat which opened on 2nd April 1883. Banking assistance was needed over the summit that was some 10 miles to the north of Beattock and 52 miles south of Glasgow Central. In the 1960s the railway provided around 150 jobs at Beattock, the village growing up around the railway's requirements for housing and other functions. The Moffat branch closed to passengers in December 1954 and to goods traffic 10 years later.

Beattock station closed to passenger traffic on 3rd January 1972 just as the line was being electrified by British Rail; its closure was to avoid the cost of raising the footbridge. It left a gap of 48 miles with no station open between Lockerbie and Carstairs. Not surprisingly there is an ongoing campaign spearheaded by the Beattock Station Action Group, which was set up in 2012 to reopen it.

The remaining sidings at Beattock are occasionally used for timber traffic.

109. The station closed in 1972. As well as being the junction for the Moffat branch it was also where banking engines were attached and detached for trains working over Beattock Summit. There is an 0-6-0 behind the fence which may be waiting for a banking turn. (J.Alsop coll.)

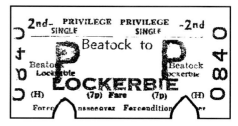

110. An unidentified 'Black 5' 4-6-0 was passing through Beattock station heading south on 6th October 1961. The Moffat branch lost its passenger services on 6th December 1954 and its freight services on 6th April 1964. (B.Brooksbank)

111.   Pickersgill 944 class 4-6-2T no. 55359 and Fairburn 4MT 2-6-4T no. 42213 were the bankers on duty on 27th June 1953. (R.Butterfield/Initial Photographics)

112.   Fairburn 4MT 2-6-4T no. 42693 provides banking assistance to the rear of the 09.25 service, from Crewe to Perth in August 1962. Princess Coronation class 4-6-2 no. 46226 *Duchess of Norfolk* was on the front. Whilst banking in steam days was dramatic, today electric locomotives and multiple units take trains up the hill at full line speed without hesitation. (W.Jamieson)

113.   Austerity class 2-10-0 no. 73794 (later no. 90770) was southbound on 1st June 1951. Goods trains as well as passenger were banked, but it was far harder to do with a loose-fitted train. No. 73794 was built for the War Department in World War II. (H.C.Casserley)

114.   Another freight comes through the station with a banker on the rear in July 1965. The lead engine was BR Standard 5MT no. 73007. This was built at Derby in 1951 and was one of the class allocated to the Scottish Region and intensively used on Glasgow to Dundee services, until these were dieselised. No. 73007 was withdrawn in March 1966. (N.Forrest/Transport Treasury)

115.   Britannia class 4-6-2 no. 70053 *Moray Firth* calls at Beattock with a train from Liverpool/ Manchester to Glasgow. CR class 439 0-4-4T no. 55232 waits in the bay platform with the 1.55pm train to Moffat on the last day of passenger services on the branch, 4th December 1954. *Moray Firth* entered service in October 1954 and was named on 2nd February 1955 and so here is running without nameplates. (W.A.C.Smith/Transport Treasury)

Beattock Shed

116.   The previous map (XXXVI) shows the location of the shed, which was north of the station and before the junction for the Moffat branch. A 45ft turntable was provided. It was replaced by a 54ft turntable in 1899. Opened in September 1847, the shed closed on 20th April 1967 and was replaced by a diesel stabling point following the elimination of steam traction north of Carlisle. In the 1970s, prior to electrification, two Class 20 locomotives were supplied by Polmadie Depot, Glasgow for banking duties when required.

   The photo shows CR class 419 0-4-4T nos 55232 and 55260 outside the shed with Fairburn 4MT 2-6-4T no. 42214 on 11th July 1956. Inside the shed on this day were no. 42213, class 812 0-6-0 no. 57568 and 0-4-4T no. 55234. (G.W.Morrison)

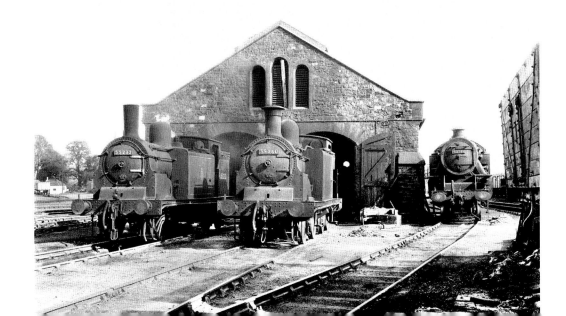

117. On 4th July 1947, LMS 4-6-2T no. 15352 was one of the banking locomotives on duty. (L.Graham/J.Alsop coll.)

118. This picture shows the shed's position relative to the station. Outside is an unidentified Fairburn 4MT 2-6-4T with another lurking inside the shed. (N.Forrest/Transport Treasury)

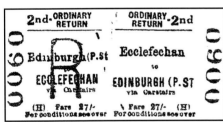

119. Class 439 0-4-4T no. 55187 was around the back of the shed on 27th June 1953. This view shows the shed extension. Withdrawn locomotives were often stored here. (R.Butterfield/Initial Photographics)

120. Another Clan class 4-6-2 is storming away from the station to attack the bank and is passing the coaling stage and water tank. A wagon, possibly a cripple requiring attention from the fitters, is in the shed whilst a BR Standard 4MT 2-6-4T waits outside in the yard. (N.Forrest/Transport Treasury)

EVOLVING THE
Vic Mitchell and Keith Smith
ULTIMATE RAIL ENCYCLOPEDIA
INTERNATIONAL

126a Camelsdale Road, GU27 3RJ. Tel:01730 813169

A-978 0 906520 B- 978 1 873793 C- 978 1 901706 D-978 1 904474
E - 978 1 906008 F - 978 1 908174 G - 978 1 910356

Our RAILWAY titles are listed below. Please check availability by looking at our website
www.middletonpress.co.uk,
telephoning us or by requesting a Brochure which includes our LATEST RAILWAY TITLES also our TRAMWAY, TROLLEYBUS, MILITARY and COASTAL series.

email:info@middletonpress.co.uk